SPECIAL REPORTS

SOCIAL MEDIA AND MODERN SOCIETY

BY KATE CONLEY

CONTENT CONSULTANT
Asta Zelenkauskaite, PhD
Associate Professor
Department of Communication
Drexel University

Essential Library
An Imprint of Abdo Publishing | abdobooks.com

abdobooks.com

Published by Abdo Publishing, a division of ABDO, PO Box 398166, Minneapolis, Minnesota 55439. Essential Library™ is a trademark and logo of Abdo Publishing.

Printed in the United States of America, North Mankato, Minnesota.
102021
012022

THIS BOOK CONTAINS RECYCLED MATERIALS

Cover Photos: iStockphoto, (girl); Shutterstock Images, (emojis)
Interior Photos: Bebeto Matthews/AP Images, 4–5; Shutterstock Images, 8, 14–15, 38–39, 42, 48–49, 51, 78–79, 90–91, 93, 98; T. Y. Lim/Shutterstock Images, 11; Antonio Guillem/Shutterstock Images, 12; Wellcome Images/Science Source, 19; Stephan Savoia/AP Images, 23; Michael Kubel/Allentown Morning Call/Tribune News Service/Getty Images, 26–27; Paul Sakuma/AP Images, 30; Manoocher Deghati/AP Images, 33; Lev Radin/Shutterstock Images, 34–35, 77, 84; Vasin Lee/Shutterstock Images, 45; Matt Gush/Shutterstock Images, 55; Tom Williams/CQ Roll Call/AP Images, 58–59; Jeffrey T. Barnes/AP Images, 61; Jonathan Ernst/Reuters/Alamy, 66–67; Nikki Kahn/The Washington Post/Getty Images, 68; Dragana Gordic/Shutterstock Images, 71; Anton Balazh/Shutterstock Images, 74; STRF/Star Max/IPx/AP Images, 86–87; Siraj Ahmad/Shutterstock Images, 88; Malte Ossowski/Sven Simon/picture-alliance/dpa/AP Images, 97

Editor: Arnold Ringstad
Series Designer: Maggie Villaume

Library of Congress Control Number: 2021941113

Publisher's Cataloging-in-Publication Data

Names: Conley, Kate, author.
Title: Social media and modern society / by Kate Conley
Description: Minneapolis, Minnesota : Abdo Publishing, 2022 | Series: Special reports | Includes online resources and index.
Identifiers: ISBN 9781532196225 (lib. bdg.) | ISBN 9781098218034 (ebook)
Subjects: LCSH: Social media and society--Juvenile literature. | Social interaction in adolescence--Juvenile literature. | Internet and teenagers--Juvenile literature. | Cell phones and teenagers--Juvenile literature. | Internet--Safety measures--Juvenile literature.
Classification: DDC 302.3--dc23

CONTENTS

Chapter One
A TECH REVOLUTION 4

Chapter Two
REMOVING THE BARRIERS OF DISTANCE AND TIME 14

Chapter Three
THE BENEFITS OF SOCIAL MEDIA 26

Chapter Four
THE ATTENTION ECONOMY 38

Chapter Five
ALGORITHMS 48

Chapter Six
HARVESTING DATA 58

Chapter Seven
FALSE STORIES 66

Chapter Eight
FREEDOM OF SPEECH 78

Chapter Nine
SOCIAL MEDIA TODAY 90

Essential Facts 100
Glossary 102
Additional Resources 104
Source Notes 106
Index 110
About the Author 112
About the Consultant 112

CHAPTER ONE

A TECH REVOLUTION

"I remember my Facebook page started getting . . . ten new followers per day," recalled Brandon Stanton, the creator of the Humans of New York (HONY) blog. "I went to Central Park with my friend . . . and I told him, 'If this keeps going like this, in three years, I'll have 10,000 Facebook fans.' And to me, that sounded like the biggest success that anyone could possibly ever imagine."[1] But Stanton had little idea of just how much he had underestimated his future.

At the time, Stanton had recently lost his job as a bond trader in Chicago. Rather than find a new job in finance, he decided to try something different. He had recently purchased a camera, and taking photos had become a new passion. So when his job ended, Stanton

The success of photographer Brandon Stanton's Humans of New York project demonstrated the power of social media.

THERMO KING

packed up his camera and moved to New York City with a project in mind. "I had this idea for a crazy, sweeping photography project," recalled Stanton. "I was going to come to New York City, photograph 10,000 people on the streets of New York, and then plot their photos on a map."[2]

Stanton moved to New York in 2010. In his first month there he took 600 photos of random people as they went about their days. He began to post them on his blog, which he linked to his Facebook account. "I had been in New York for a few months, and I had been doing it every single day, trying to get traction, trying to get something going, and it really wasn't working. . . . It's very hard to get that first core group of fans."[3]

At the same time that Stanton was looking for an audience, a tech revolution was happening across the nation. Social media was spreading quickly. It had once been a realm for college students and computer fanatics. But now

FACEBOOK

Many social media sites have been created over the years. By far the largest and most influential has been Facebook. In 2020, 2.8 billion users logged on to the platform at least once a month.[4] In the United States, approximately 70 percent of adults used Facebook. Of those users, about three-quarters signed in each day.[5] Many used it not only for connecting with friends but also for news and entertainment.

services like Facebook, YouTube, Tumblr, Twitter, and Pinterest were catching on with a growing number of people. These sites were going mainstream. And as social media grew, so did Stanton's career. The HONY Facebook page gathered millions of followers in subsequent years.

GROWING QUICKLY

The Pew Research Center began keeping statistics on social media use in 2005. That year, only 5 percent of American adults used social media. As word of these services spread and technology made them more accessible, the number of users grew quickly. In 2011, the figure had risen to half of all Americans. In 2019 nearly three-quarters of American adults were using social media.[6]

A NEW WAY TO SHARE

The path Stanton followed to success was a new one. Social media changed how people share information. A photographer like Stanton no longer needed an agent, a gallery show, or a publisher to share his work. Instead, social media allowed him to put his content on a platform himself. Placing his content on Facebook was free, and anyone could access it. Never in human history had sharing information with a global audience been so easy and cheap. David Karp, the founder of Tumblr and a fan of HONY, explained Stanton's success by saying,

Social media gives individual users the power to steer trends, shift online conversations, and affect the culture like never before.

"Creative work like this used to need to be blessed by big institutions to get it in front of a big audience, but this guy built the audience himself."[7]

Modern social media platforms arose in the early 2000s, growing out of earlier social networking sites from the 1990s. These platforms allowed users to be active participants online, rather than just consumers of information. Social media platforms formed user networks, which provided new opportunities. They allowed users to communicate directly with other people on the site. People gained the power to share a variety of content, including text, images, and videos, with other people in their networks. Users could interact with the content by leaving comments or sharing it with others.

"SOCIAL NETWORKS REPRESENT THE DIGITAL REFLECTION OF WHAT HUMANS DO: WE CONNECT AND SHARE."[8]

—JEREMIAH OWYANG, LEADER AND ANALYST IN THE TECH INDUSTRY

Today's social media has three basic characteristics. The combination of these traits is what makes social media different from other sites on the internet. The first characteristic is the ability for users to both share and receive content. The second feature is active participation. A social media site grows in usefulness and influence as more people actively use it. The third characteristic is an ability to spread information quickly. Content posted on social media can go viral, reaching a worldwide audience of millions shortly after being published.

SOCIAL MEDIA AROUND THE WORLD

Facebook and Twitter are popular in the United States and elsewhere in the world. But many countries have their own social networking services. The messaging application WeChat has an enormous base of users in China. The social networking service VK is widely used in Russia. Some nations ban US social media services from operating within their borders. China has banned Facebook, Twitter, Instagram, Pinterest, Snapchat, and many other services.

GROWING PAINS

Social media grew quickly in the 2000s and 2010s. That growth provided users with many benefits. They have connected with family and friends, met new people, and expressed themselves in ways that were unimaginable in the past. But it has also come with its share of problems.

Some of those problems have affected society as a whole. Users can share anything they like, whether or not it is true. Some stories with false information go viral. And it can be difficult to tell which stories are false, even for savvy users. The spread of false information can have harmful effects on society.

Other problems with social media center around the tech companies that run these platforms. These companies

FAKE NEWS & FREE SPEECH

Fake news and false information have a reputation for running unchecked on social media sites. They often spread faster than true information. In a 2019 survey, Americans revealed that they thought fake news stories were a larger problem than terrorism, climate change, and racism. These fake news stories reduce the confidence Americans have in the government, as well as in one another. Eighty percent of adults surveyed wanted steps taken to restrict fake news, though it was unclear who would do the restricting. In contrast, 20 percent believed these fake news stories should be protected as free speech.[9]

People have accused major social media platforms of censorship for suspending or banning certain accounts.

have come under fire for some of their actions. They hold valuable data about each user. Selling this data is profitable for them. But critics argue selling data violates the privacy of the users. Sometimes hackers illegally steal personal data from these companies, leaving users vulnerable to fraud and other problems. Some companies, such as Facebook and Twitter, have shut down accounts that were spreading messages the companies deemed

For some people, overuse of social media can be harmful to their happiness and mental health.

harmful. Opponents argue this restriction of users is unfair and wrong.

Social media can have problematic effects on individuals too. The growth of social media has led to concerns about how people spend their time. Many people use social media for several hours each day. This can increase a user's risk for depression and anxiety. It contributes to feelings of isolation and inadequacy.

A person may start to feel a fear of missing out on the experiences others are having, commonly known as FOMO. People can also become addicted to social media. It can affect the brain in a similar way to drugs, gambling, and other addictive behaviors.

These negative effects have caused many people to reassess the role of social media in their lives. Figuring out how to balance the benefits of social media with its downsides will be an ongoing issue for the foreseeable future. To many people, there is a battle for truth, power, freedom, and well-being happening online, and citizens of the world must grapple with it each time they log in to social media.

"SOCIAL MEDIA IS THE ULTIMATE EQUALIZER. LENDS A VOICE & PLATFORM TO ANYONE WILLING TO ENGAGE. ALSO LENDS INFINITE OPPORTUNITIES & CHALLENGES."[10]

– TWEET BY AMY JO MARTIN, AUTHOR AND ENTREPRENEUR

CHAPTER TWO

REMOVING THE BARRIERS OF DISTANCE AND TIME

In 2020, nearly half the world's population logged on to social media sites. The ability to connect with others has driven this surge in users. Social media makes communicating cheap and instant. When a person shares a photo with friends on social media, those friends can see it immediately no matter where in the world they are located. Social media has removed distance and time as barriers to connecting people.

This rapid, real-time communication is a relatively new development. In early American history, people

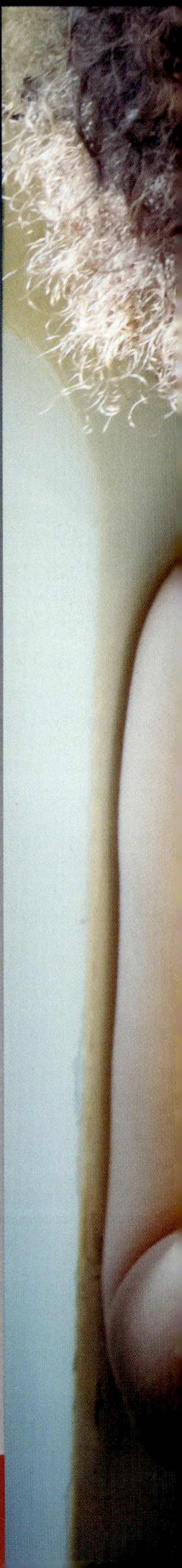

Social media services have made it possible to communicate instantly with friends on the other side of the planet.

wrote letters to exchange news and stay in touch. Messengers on horseback delivered the letters. Depending on the distance, it could take a messenger days to deliver a letter. And to send a message overseas required ships. A single voyage could take months to complete. The result was that news spread at a slow pace.

Inventors tried many ways to speed up the spread of information. They experimented with encoding messages through sound and sight. These were improvements over horseback messengers but still had many drawbacks. Visual signals, such as flag-based codes, could not be used in the dark or during foggy weather. Many inventors sought to create new communication methods using electricity. American Samuel Morse had the first widespread success with one of these devices, the telegraph, in 1844.

THE OPTICAL TELEGRAPH

The precursor to the electric telegraph relied on visuals. French brothers Claude and Ignace Chappe created a visual signaling system in 1791. It involved a series of towers on hilltops between three and six miles (5 and 10 km) apart. Each tower had a beam with two movable arms. The arm positions matched numbers and letters in a codebook. The operator would set the arms to send a signal to the next tower down the line. There, an operator with binoculars would read the signal, make the arms on his tower match, and send it to the next tower. By the 1830s, nearly 1,000 towers connected the major cities of Europe.

MORE TO THE STORY

DEMONSTRATING THE TELEGRAPH

Samuel Morse faced skepticism from the public about his invention. Many Americans considered the telegraph to be foolish and crazy. Morse needed a way to prove its usefulness. In December 1842, he convinced Congress to provide him $30,000 to build an experimental telegraph line.[1] It ran from Baltimore, Maryland, to Washington, DC. Morse and his partner Alfred Vail demonstrated the line on May 1, 1844. It had not yet been fully completed, but Morse saw an opportunity. Baltimore was hosting the Whig National Convention. This political party was selecting its presidential candidate. Vail, who was near Baltimore, telegraphed the news of the winner to Morse, who was in Washington. At the same time, a messenger carried the announcement to Washington by train. The messenger arrived 64 minutes after the telegraph message. Morse had successfully demonstrated that electricity could carry news far faster than even a train.

NEW TECHNOLOGY CREATES CONNECTIONS

Morse's first telegraph line went from Baltimore, Maryland, to Washington, DC. One electrical wire connected the two terminals. To send a message, an operator in one city pressed a key connected to the wire. When this happened, a pulse of electrical current made an arm on the other city's receiver press downward. The arm made a long or short mark on a roll of paper each time it moved. A short mark was called a dot, and a long mark was called a dash. Each letter in the alphabet was represented by a unique combination of dots and dashes. This is known as Morse code. An operator at the receiving end translated the code into letters and words.

"IT WOULD NOT BE LONG ERE THE WHOLE SURFACE OF THE COUNTRY WOULD BE CHANNELED FOR THOSE NERVES WHICH ARE TO DIFFUSE, WITH THE SPEED OF THOUGHT, A KNOWLEDGE OF ALL THAT IS OCCURRING THROUGHOUT THE LAND, MAKING, IN FACT, ONE NEIGHBORHOOD OF THE WHOLE COUNTRY."[3]

—SAMUEL MORSE

By 1850, the United States had 12,000 miles (19,300 km) of telegraph wire.[2] Telegraph engineers wondered whether it could be used to send messages between

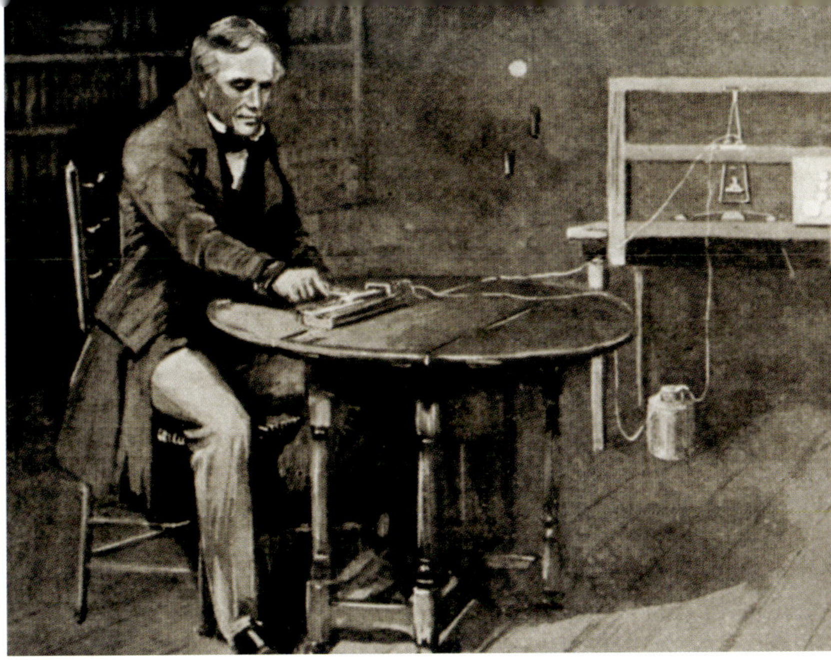

Samuel Morse's telegraph sparked a revolution in sharing information.

continents too. To test the idea, workers laid thousands of miles of insulated telegraph wire on the floor of the Atlantic Ocean. The line between Europe and North America began operating in 1858. It made communication between the two continents dramatically faster than ever before.

As the system grew, the telegraph itself was simplified. Rather than drawing dots and dashes on paper, telegraphs began using sounders. These devices made clicking noises for the dots and dashes. Skilled telegraph operators could decode a message by ear and respond quickly. This method made real-time conversations over great distances possible for the first time in history. The telegraph had overcome the obstacle of distance, making the world a much smaller place.

CREATING NEW NETWORKS

The telephone was another new technology that created social networks. In 1876, Alexander Graham Bell invented the telephone. It allowed people to speak to one another in real time over great distances. At first, telephones were mainly used by businesses. It didn't take long for telephone companies to expand their market. "They realized, 'We can make money off gossip and idle conversation and sociability on the telephone,'" said Claude Fischer, author of *America Calling*.[4] By 1910, the United States had a network of 5.8 million telephones.[5]

THE FIRST CHAT ROOMS

During quiet times, operators sent telegraph messages to one another. They formed friendships, held meetings, traded jokes, fell in love, gossiped, and played checkers all through Morse code. "When a wire connected several telegraph stations, all the operators along the line could hear everything that was transmitted and join in the unofficial banter, in effect occupying a single, shared chat room," author Tom Standage explained in his book *Writing on the Wall*.[6] And just as today's users have shorthand such as BRB, LOL, and AFK, telegraph operators used abbreviations to make transmissions quicker. For example, "I I" meant "I am ready," "S F D" meant "stop for dinner," and "1" meant "wait a moment." To identify themselves, operators had unique two-letter signatures, an early form of the handles used online today.

For the next several decades, the telephone, the telegraph, and handwritten letters were the main ways to connect people over great distances. Other technologies, such as the radio and the television, also created forms of social networks during this time. But they were passive. People could not broadcast a radio program or television show from their own homes to the homes of their friends. Instead, people could watch or listen only to the content that networks broadcasted. This basic arrangement of media remained relatively stable for decades.

In the 1960s, things began to change. At that time, the United States and the Soviet Union were enemies in the Cold War. In this long-standing national rivalry, the two countries built up large military forces but never directly fought one another. Some leaders worried the Soviet Union might bomb the United States. As a defensive measure, the United States wanted to develop a decentralized way to network its computers together. If a nuclear attack destroyed a military base and its computers, messages could be routed through other computers on the network. By the late 1960s, the US government had created the Advanced Research Projects Agency

Network (ARPANET). It linked computers across the country through telephone lines.

RAYMOND TOMLINSON AND EMAIL

Raymond Tomlinson began developing email as an experiment. Programmers could send messages between computers, but it was an inefficient process. Tomlinson thought there was a better way. "At the time there was no really good way to leave messages for people," recalled Tomlinson. "The telephone worked up to a point, but someone had to be there to receive the call. And if it wasn't the person you wanted to get, it was an administrative assistant or an answering service or something of that sort. That was the mechanism you had to go through to leave a message, so everyone latched onto the idea that you could leave messages on the computer."[7] With his experiment, Tomlinson ultimately connected millions of users throughout the world.

The ARPANET became the forerunner of today's internet. It allowed users to transfer data between computers on the network. As technology improved, other computer networks began to form. A computer scientist named Raymond Tomlinson developed the software to send messages between networked computers. In 1971, he sent the first email. Computers found widespread use at universities in this era. By 1979, a network called USENET allowed computers to send messages between Duke University and the University of North Carolina. It soon spread to other colleges.

MODERN SOCIAL NETWORKS

These early networks were closed systems. Computers could speak to one another if they were in the same network. But they could not communicate with computers outside of the network. That all changed in 1991 with the introduction of the World Wide Web, invented by researcher Tim Berners-Lee. The web is a system that allows users to create pages connected by clickable links. Software programs called web browsers are used to access it via the internet. The release of the popular web browser Mosaic in 1993 helped make the web mainstream. When that happened, the internet grew quickly. Within a few

Tim Berners-Lee's World Wide Web laid the groundwork for social media services.

years, the forerunners of modern social networks began to appear.

Early internet sites were largely passive. Users could read content that others posted, but the ability to interact with that content was limited. Some sites began to experiment with how to change that. One of those sites was called SixDegrees. A developer named Andrew Weinreich launched the site in May 1997. It is widely considered to be the first social media site. SixDegrees allowed users to create a profile, keep a list of friends, and communicate with them through private messages. By 2000, the site had three million users.[8]

Following the success of SixDegrees, developers began to launch other social media sites, including Friendster, LinkedIn, and Match.com. One of the most successful services during this period was called Myspace. It began in 2003 and quickly drew a large pool of young users who were between the ages of 14 and 34. Users created personalized profile pages, built networks of friends, and shared music, videos, and blog posts. They could also send instant messages and comment on content. By the end of 2005, the site had more than 26.7 million users.[9]

Myspace reigned as the world's largest social media site until 2008, when Facebook overtook it. A Harvard University student named Mark Zuckerberg had launched Facebook in 2004 to connect Harvard students. Within two weeks, half of the student body had signed up for the site. Its popularity spread to other colleges and high schools. Demand increased, so in September 2006 Facebook opened registration to anyone over age 13 with an email address. The result was an explosion of growth. By the time it overtook Myspace in 2008, Facebook had 100 million users.[10] It had become the undisputed leader in social media.

MARK ZUCKERBERG

Mark Zuckerberg was born in White Plains, New York, on May 14, 1984. Even as a child, he found computers fascinating. At age 12, he used a home computer to program what he called Zucknet. It was a messaging system that allowed family members to communicate from one room to another in their house. He also spent time making computer games with friends. His skills as a programmer grew. In high school, Zuckerberg created music sharing software called Synapse. Major companies, such as AOL and Microsoft, wanted to buy it and hire Zuckerberg before he graduated from high school. Zuckerberg chose to go to Harvard instead. By his sophomore year, he had founded what would become the world's largest social network.

CHAPTER THREE

THE BENEFITS OF SOCIAL MEDIA

On March 2, 2014, a Pennsylvania woman named Katheryn Deprill made a bold decision. Deprill had been adopted as an infant, and she wanted to find her birth mother. Brenda Hollis, Deprill's adoptive mother, suggested she use social media to reach her birth mother. "I said, 'Why don't you put it on Facebook just for fun and see what happens?'" recalled Hollis.[1]

So, Deprill did just that. She posted a photo on Facebook with details about her birth story. In the photo, Deprill stood behind a handwritten sign that said: "Looking for my birth mother. She gave birth to me

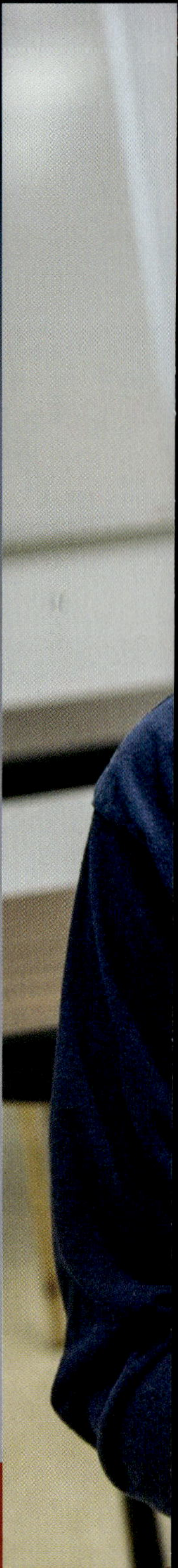

Katheryn Deprill used the immense reach of social media to find her birth mother, illustrating how the scale of online services can make new things possible.

Newborn infant abandoned in Allentown restaurant
9-14-86
A baby girl, described by Allentown police as being "hours-old," was found abandoned early yesterday in a restroom of a South Side fast-food restaurant.
Police said the baby was found at about 8:14 a.m. in the Burger King Restaurant at 1958 S. 4th St. They said a customer, identified only as Libby Landis, had just sat down in a restaurant booth when she heard the sound of a crying baby coming from the restroom.
Landis, police said, went into the restroom and found the baby on the floor, wrapped in a red sweater.
She contacted Burger King employee Robert Wilson, who notified police.
The baby was taken by city ambulance to Allentown Hospital, where aides later said, "Baby Doe is in satisfactory condition." The baby is 6 pounds 15½ ounces and 21 inches long.
Lehigh County Children & Youth Service later took custody of the baby. A spokesman said the agency in such cases "generally takes custody and, when the child is medically able, places the infant in foster care."
Police are asking for help in trying to identify the baby's mother.
Anyone with information on the possible identity of the mother, a Caucasian, is asked to contact police headquarters at 437-7721. All calls will be confidential.

September 15th, 1986. She abandoned me in the Burger King bathroom only hours old, Allentown, PA. Please help me find her by sharing my post. Maybe she will see this. Thank you."

The post took off quickly. Facebook users shared it more than 33,000 times, and the story gained national attention. All of that attention paid off. Three weeks later, Deprill and her birth mother were reunited for the first time. "I have literally not wiped the smile off my face," said Deprill after meeting her birth mother. "I never in a million years thought I'd find her."[2]

TEENS AND CONNECTIONS

In 2018, the Pew Research Center conducted a survey of teenagers, asking for their views on social media use. Teens were asked to rate whether social media had a positive, neutral, or negative effect on people their age. Most teens said social media was either positive (31 percent) or neutral (45 percent). Many respondents cited connection as the biggest positive aspect of social media. "I feel that social media can make people my age feel less lonely or alone. It creates a space where you can interact with people," said a 15-year-old female respondent. A male respondent of the same age said, "It enables people to connect with friends easily and be able to make new friends as well."[3]

MAKING CONNECTIONS

The connection Deprill made with her birth mother is just one example of the positive effects of social media. And in social media's early years, that focus on connecting people was its main objective. It wasn't about selling products, raising advertising revenue, or gaining political power. Social media was about using technology to connect people in new ways that would have been impossible to imagine just a generation earlier.

"It's easy today to lose sight of the fact that these tools actually have created some wonderful things in the world," says Tim Kendall in the documentary *The Social Dilemma*. He served as president of Pinterest and director of monetization at Facebook. "They've reunited lost family members. They've found organ donors. I mean, there were meaningful systemic changes happening around the world because of these platforms that were positive!"[4]

"THE INTERNET IS PROVING TO BE ONE OF THE MOST POWERFUL AMPLIFIERS OF SPEECH EVER INVENTED. IT OFFERS A GLOBAL MEGAPHONE FOR VOICES THAT MIGHT OTHERWISE BE HEARD ONLY FEEBLY, IF AT ALL. IT INVITES AND FACILITATES MULTIPLE POINTS OF VIEW AND DIALOGUE IN WAYS UNIMPLEMENTABLE BY TRADITIONAL, ONE-WAY MEDIA."[5]

— VINTON CERF, AMERICAN COMPUTER SCIENTIST WHO IS CONSIDERED ONE OF THE FOUNDERS OF THE INTERNET

In 2019 Facebook celebrated its fifteenth anniversary. To mark the occasion, founder Mark Zuckerberg wrote a post on his own Facebook profile reflecting on all that had

Mark Zuckerberg has described the desire to connect people as a driving force for Facebook since its early years.

happened in that time. The world of social media had undergone dramatic changes over that decade and a half, but Zuckerberg came back to the topic that had driven him to build the site in the first place: connection.

"At the time, it struck me that there were many websites to find almost anything—books, music, news, information, businesses—except for what actually matters most: people," Zuckerberg wrote in his post. "So I built a simple website organized around people, where we could connect with the people we wanted and share what was important to us. This desire to express ourselves, learn about each other, and connect in new ways was greater than I'd imagined."[6]

As social media has developed and grown in the years since then, it has created connections in a variety of ways. LinkedIn has brought together job seekers with open positions. Users on Facebook, Twitter, Instagram, TikTok, and YouTube have built communities across the globe that are linked by common interests. Various dating social networks have led to countless relationships and marriages. And it's not just about meeting new people. Social media has allowed families and friends who are separated by great distances to keep in touch easily. It has transformed the way people think about connecting with one another.

BUILDING SOCIAL NETWORKS

Social media sites employ strategies to connect people with one another. Twitter added a feature in 2016 called the "Connect tab." It suggests people and groups to follow that may appeal to users based on the accounts they already follow. In much the same way, Facebook has a feature called "People You May Know," Instagram has "Suggested for You," and TikTok has "For You." All of these features recommend people to follow based on a user's interests. Though each platform uses a different name for this feature, they all have the same goal: to connect people and build larger networks of users.

SPARKING REVOLUTION

Social media forms more than just connections between

friends and family. It can also form connections among members of a wider community. Those connections allow people to organize in ways that would have looked much different in the past. The Arab Spring was one of the most visible examples of this. It was a series of pro-democracy protests in the Middle East and North Africa in 2010 and 2011. These were some of the earliest political protests to rely on social media as a form of widespread communication and coordination.

One of the people leading the charge on social media was Wael Ghonim. He is an activist and computer scientist from Egypt. At the time of the Arab Spring, Hosni Mubarak was Egypt's leader. He had been president for nearly 30 years. Though he had technically been elected by the people, many Egyptians considered him a dictator. They were unhappy with the way he had run the country. When Mubarak's police forces killed an innocent man named Khaled Said, Ghonim had had enough.

In June 2010, Ghonim created an anonymous Facebook group called "We Are All Khaled Said." It quickly drew the attention of hundreds of thousands of others who were unhappy with Mubarak. In January 2011, a coup in Tunisia

Protests in Egypt, organized in part on Facebook, sought to remove the nation's unpopular leader from office.

ousted that nation's dictator, Zine al-Abidine Ben Ali. Ghonim wondered whether Facebook could aid in making the same thing happen in Egypt.

"What I did was just basically put the invitation on a page that has hundreds of thousands of followers, and that ended up—the event on Facebook reached a million people and it was confirmed by 100,000. We took to the streets . . . it showed to me the great power of social media," said Ghonim of the protests that followed his January 2011 post.[7] Following a series of major protests, Mubarak stepped down as president in February 2011, and a new government was established.

FROM THE HEADLINES

#METOO

Tarana Burke was a youth worker at a camp when a girl named Heaven approached her. The girl wanted to tell an adult about sexual abuse she had experienced. Burke was shaken by Heaven's story and sent her away. But she felt guilty for her reaction and kept asking herself, "Why couldn't you just say, 'me too?'"[8] Not long after, Burke began to speak out against sexual violence. She created a Myspace page in 2006 called "Me Too" to help others. Her work focused on her local community until 2017.

On October 5 of that year, a news story accused Hollywood mogul Harvey Weinstein of decades of serial sexual abuse. Actress Alyssa Milano wanted to draw more attention to the problem. On October 15 she posted, "If you've been sexually harassed or assaulted write 'me too' as a reply to this tweet."[9] The post went viral, and thousands of people responded to her. The hashtag #MeToo lit up social media around the world. Milano's tweet not only amplified the Weinstein discussion but also further advanced Burke's work. From the Myspace beginnings to Milano's viral tweet, social media had propelled a global movement of women. "My hope is people will get the idea of the magnitude, of

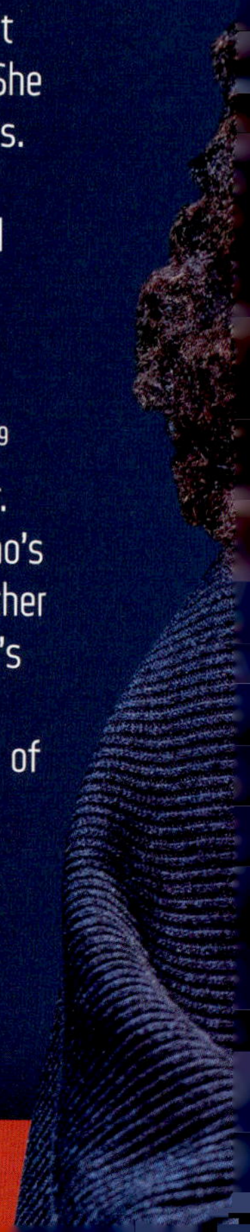

Tarana Burke spearheaded the #MeToo movement.

just how many people have been affected by this in the world, in our lifetimes, in this country," Milano said. "The most important thing that it did was to shift the conversation away from the predator and to the victim."[10]

DELIVERING AID

The Arab Spring was just one example of how social media could connect communities. A natural disaster in the United States provided yet another opportunity to use social media in an entirely new way. Hurricane Harvey hit Texas in August 2017. The devastation was widespread. More than 60 inches (152 cm) of rain fell in some parts of Texas, leaving hundreds of thousands of homes and cars flooded. It was one of the most devastating rainfall events in US history. As floodwaters rose, people reached out for help, but emergency services were overwhelmed by demand. Looking for alternatives, many residents turned to social media.

Maritza Ritz Willis was one of the hurricane's victims who was searching for help. When the 911 phone service did not respond, she instead posted

MOBILIZING MOVEMENTS

In 2011, the Dubai School of Government released the Arab Social Media Report, which detailed how social media was shaping the protests in the region. The report noted that between January and April 2011, Facebook underwent explosive growth in the region, more than doubling in size in those four months. As more people joined the site, the protests gained momentum. Nearly nine out of ten Egyptians and Tunisians surveyed for the report said they were using Facebook either to spread awareness of the cause or to organize protests.

to Twitter: "I have 2 children with me and tge [sic] water is swallowing us up. Please send help."[11] Someone saw her message and organized help. About an hour later, Willis and her children had been rescued.

SAFETY CHECK

In 2011, an earthquake triggered a tsunami in Japan. More than 20,000 people died during the tsunami and its aftermath. Facebook leaders wanted to figure out how social media could help in disasters like this one. Their engineers began to design features to make communicating during a disaster easier. In 2014, Facebook released Safety Check. It becomes activated when a user is in an area where a natural disaster occurs. It allows users to mark themselves as safe. That information is then posted to the user's news feed for his or her entire network of friends to see.

Hurricane Harvey was not the first time that social media had been used in natural disasters. But the way people used it was different, according to Nikki Usher, a media professor at George Washington University. "We've seen disasters through Facebook where you can mark yourself safe and there have been movements toward giving people a chance to check in—but this is one of the first real disasters where you see rescuing via social media, you see images that the media couldn't possibly get," said Usher.[12] As social media grows, the ways in which it can help society will continue to grow with it.

CHAPTER FOUR

THE ATTENTION ECONOMY

Social media has created connections that would have been unthinkable just a generation ago. But it also has a darker side. It has created an online economy based on a user's attention. "There's a hidden goal driving the direction of all of the technology we make, and that goal is the race for our attention," says Tristan Harris. Harris is a computer scientist, ethicist, and cofounder of the Center for Humane Technology. "News site[s], TED [talks], elections, politicians, games, even meditation apps have to compete for one thing, which is our attention and there's only so much of it."[1]

This aspect of social media is like one giant game. A user has a fixed amount of attention to devote to social media each day. Capturing that user's attention

Social media services seek to capture the attention of users and keep them coming back.

for as long as possible is the objective for social media platforms. To succeed, platforms must keep their users online. The more time users spend scrolling, the more money social media platforms make. Winning this attention war can mean billions of dollars in profit.

Traditional tech companies sell hardware and software to make their money. But social networking platforms offered a free service, and to keep it running they needed a way to monetize it. To make this happen, social media leaders looked to Google. Google, a giant in the world of online search engines, had innovated a new kind of business model. Like social media sites, Google was free. In exchange for the free search service, the user viewed ads. Advertisers who wanted to show their product to a Google user had

GOOGLE

Google began as a search engine created by Sergey Brin and Larry Page in 1998. It started in Page's dorm room at Stanford University. Brin and Page wanted to create a way to search through the rapidly increasing number of websites. They created a search algorithm that ranked sites. A page linked to lots of other pages would be ranked higher than one with fewer connections. There were other search engines available at the time, such as Ask Jeeves and Yahoo! But Google's algorithm proved so useful that it overtook them all. By 2004, users were making more than 200 million searches on Google each day. In 2021, most of the world's online searches were made on Google.

to pay Google a fee. Those fees helped make Google a multibillion-dollar business.

GOOGLE'S EXAMPLE

"Everyone in 2006, including all of us at Facebook, just had total admiration for Google and what Google had built," recalled Tim Kendall.[2] He worked as the director of monetization at Facebook from 2006 to 2010. His job was to figure out how to make Facebook's business profitable. "[Google] was this incredibly useful service that did, as far as we could tell, lots of goodness for the world, and they built this parallel money machine. We had such envy for that, and it seemed so elegant to us and so perfect."[3]

In 2007, Facebook introduced Facebook Ads, which had three parts. First, businesses could build their own pages. Second, a system would spread ads through the social network. And third, an interface would gather data on users that would be useful to advertisers. "For the last hundred years media has been pushed out to people, but now marketers are going to be a part of the conversation," Zuckerberg explained when Facebook Ads launched.

Advertising on social media is all about capitalizing on the attention of a service's users.

"And they're going to do this by using the social graph in the same way our users do."[4]

This model turned traditional ideas of customers and products upside down. Facebook's product was not its social media site. Rather, its product was the attention of its users, and its customers were the advertisers. The advertisers were willing to pay money to put their products in front of Facebook's users. That monetized the service. It is how Facebook made billions of dollars but kept its site free for users.

Because their customers are advertisers, social media platforms want to keep advertisers happy. They want those advertisers to keep coming back and paying fees. To make that happen, social media platforms offer them something that other forms of advertising do not have: data about the people who see their ads. To gather data, social media sites monitor every action, every click, and every post. "They know when people are lonely. They know when people are depressed. They know when people are looking at photos of [their] ex-romantic partners. They know what you're doing late at night. They know the entire thing," says Harris.[5]

ZUCKERBERG ON USER DATA

Mark Zuckerberg testified about how Facebook uses data in a hearing before Congress in 2018. Lawmakers wanted to know whether user data was being sold. Zuckerberg responded to the questions by saying, "What we allow is for advertisers to tell us who they want to reach, and then we do the placement. So, if an advertiser comes to us and says, 'All right, I am a ski shop and I want to sell skis to women,' then we might have some sense, because people shared skiing-related content, or said they were interested in that, they shared whether they're a woman, and then we can show the ads to the right people without that data ever changing hands and going to the advertiser."[6] In other words, Facebook does not sell user data. Instead, it acts as an intermediary between users and advertisers by collecting user data and then using it to help other businesses sell goods.

Knowing all that information is valuable to advertisers. Imagine a group of four friends: A, B, C, and D. The social media site tracks that friends A and B have both bought a product and written positive comments about it.

That provides the product's advertisers with valuable information. Users C and D are more likely to buy the product because their friends bought it and liked it. As a result, the advertisers can focus their money on showing ads to users C and D. This ad placement has an increased chance of turning into a sale. Advertisers are willing to pay social media sites big money for this kind of precise targeting.

TEENS AND MEDIA

As social media sites become increasingly engineered to be addictive, many parents and educators have a growing concern about how they are affecting the nation's youth. In 2019, the nonprofit group Common Sense released a study about the online habits of Americans between 13 and 18 years of age. Just over two-thirds of the teens spent more than four hours online each day. The most common activity was watching videos. Seventy percent said they watched videos online every day, with YouTube being the preferred platform. Videos were followed in popularity by gaming and social media platforms. Teens who grow addicted to social media may spend increasingly long periods of time on it. They may rely on it to feel good about themselves. When this happens, the teen's real-life relationships often suffer in favor of online relationships.

PULLING USERS DEEPER INTO THE SITE

Social media platforms wanted to keep advertisers happy. As the sites matured, they sought new ways to keep users on their sites for longer periods of time so they could show more ads. That came in the form of new features to the platforms to make these sites more addictive. "It's as if they're

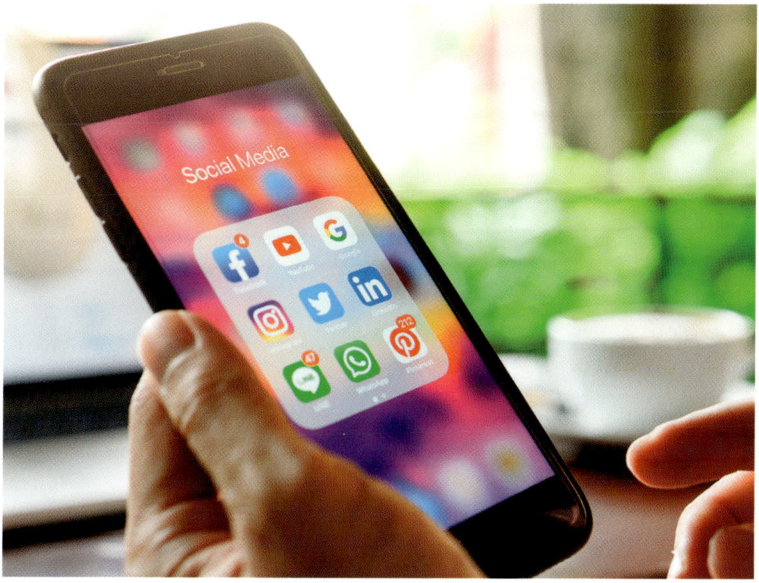

Red notification badges are one method of drawing users back into social media apps.

taking behavioral cocaine and just sprinkling it all over your interface and that's the thing that keeps you coming back," said programmer Aza Raskin.[7]

Raskin designed one of those addictive features himself. He invented what is known as "infinite scroll." It works by continually and automatically loading new content as users scroll through their news feeds. The service keeps seamlessly feeding content to users. But that's not the only feature that aids people in spending time on social media. Likes on Facebook, hearts on Twitter and Instagram, and Autoplay on YouTube are just a few of the features that keep users coming back for more.

MORE TO THE STORY

CHAMATH PALIHAPITIYA

The tactics social media has used to attract and addict users have come under scrutiny in recent years. Chamath Palihapitiya worked at Facebook from 2007 to 2011 as its vice president of user growth. After he left Facebook, Palihapitiya became one of social media's most outspoken critics. In a 2017 interview, he said he felt "tremendous guilt" for his role in growing social media. "I think we have created tools that are ripping apart the social fabric of how society works," he said.[8] He directly addressed the psychology of how this happens though the use of likes, hearts, and other responses that produce a dopamine hit for users. Dopamine is a chemical released in the brain that is connected to feelings of pleasure. "The short-term, dopamine-driven feedback loops that we have created are destroying how society works. No civil discourse, no cooperation, misinformation, mistruth," said Palihapitiya.[9] He has stopped using social media himself, and his biggest advice for others was to take a hard break from it too.

"Behind every screen on your phone, there are generally like literally a thousand engineers that have worked on this thing to try to make it maximally addicting," said Raskin.[10]

Sean Parker, who served as Facebook's first president, explained it in similar terms. Programmers created a feedback loop to pull users deeper into the site. For example, a user makes a post that get likes and comments. The user wants more of that positive feedback and so posts more content. And as the new content gets responses, it spurs the user to post more. It creates a never-ending loop fueled by likes and comments. Social media leaders knew this. They were "exploiting a vulnerability in human psychology," according to Parker. "The inventors, creators . . . understood this consciously. And we did it anyway."[11]

ADDICTION AND MONEY

Jaron Lanier, author of *Ten Arguments for Deleting Your Social Media Accounts Right Now*, has compared social media to smoking. "We've had mass addictions in the past that were connected to commercial interests. It used to be that people smoked everywhere and everyone was addicted to cigarettes—thought they were cool—so it was impossible to have a conversation about doing away with them," said Lanier. "And then finally, there were enough people who weren't addicted for us to have a conversation, and we realized—'Hey, this is stupid; we should at least not have cigarettes in public places.' And it really helped the world. . . . The difference, in this case, is that the side effect [of social media addiction] is to disconnect humanity from reality."[12]

CHAPTER FIVE

ALGORITHMS

As Facebook gained popularity, many users began to build large networks of friends. The growth created a problem. To see what a friend had posted, a user had to go to that person's profile. It was time consuming and inconvenient. To solve this problem, Facebook introduced the news feed in 2006. It created a central place to see updates from friends. But the news feed was not just a list of posts in chronological order. An algorithm decided which posts showed up in each user's news feed.

An algorithm is a set of step-by-step instructions to reach a specific goal. Some algorithms are simple, such as following a recipe or solving a multiplication problem. Others are more complex creations of computer programming. They can organize large quantities of data efficiently. Social media sites use

People using social media services see feeds of content that algorithms tailor to their interests.

Social Network
Alex
Events
Friends
Posts
Bookmarks
Products
Photos
Events
Anna Hicks
Hi everyone! Check out our new art studio in the city center!
Messenger
Sam Johns
Marta Stevenson
Kevin Charles
Lauren Moore
Pages
Eco Life
Follow
Arts and More
Follow
Healthy Eating

algorithms to predict what content a user wants to see in a news feed. They pare down massive amounts of content, personalizing the news feed that each user sees. Algorithms are designed to give users a relevant, meaningful, customized experience on social media.

To make accurate predictions, algorithms need data. This data comes from the users themselves. Social media services track each user's habits. "What I want people to know is that everything they're doing online is being watched, is being tracked, is being measured," said Jeff Seibert, a former Twitter executive. "Every single action you take is carefully monitored and recorded. Exactly what image you stop and look at, for how long you look at it."[1] The more data an algorithm has, the better it is at making predictions.

A CLOSELY GUARDED SECRET

The specific details of the algorithms used by each social media site are a mystery to users. Each site uses different algorithms that are tweaked frequently, and the companies closely guard this information. Social media algorithms are often considered a trade secret, similar to the formula for Coca-Cola or the recipe for KFC's blend of spices. The information the algorithms collect is valuable. Social media companies use it to keep users on their sites longer, and the longer a user is on a site, the more money a company can make.

A SHIFT IN INFORMATION FLOW

Data tracking and algorithms made news feeds more streamlined and convenient. However, this shift came with some unintended consequences. As people used social media sites more often and for longer periods, the algorithms had more data than ever before. This allowed the algorithms to make better and better predictions. They became so good at it that they often eliminated content that might disagree with a user's viewpoint. They increasingly fed users the posts that were likely to align with their own beliefs.

By feeding users only content they are likely to agree with, algorithms can worsen political divides.

"THE POWER OF INDIVIDUAL TARGETING—THE TECHNOLOGY WILL BE SO GOOD IT WILL BE VERY HARD FOR PEOPLE TO WATCH OR CONSUME SOMETHING THAT HAS NOT IN SOME SENSE BEEN TAILORED FOR THEM."[2]

— ERIC SCHMIDT, FORMER GOOGLE CEO

"There's this kind of shift in how information is flowing online, and it's invisible. And if we don't pay attention to it, it could be a real problem," said author and activist Eli Pariser in a 2011 TED Talk called "Beware of Online Filter Bubbles." Pariser first noticed this shift in his Facebook news feed in connection with politics. Pariser identifies as a liberal. But he followed a number of conservative friends on Facebook. "I like hearing what they're thinking about," said Pariser. "I like seeing what they link to—I like learning a thing or two. And so I was surprised when I noticed one day that the conservatives had disappeared from my Facebook feed."

Pariser was experiencing the effects of an algorithm. "What it turned out was going on was that Facebook was looking at which links I clicked on, and it was noticing that, actually, I was clicking more on my liberal friends' links than on my conservative friends' links. And without consulting me about it, it had edited them out. They disappeared." The algorithms had tracked his habits and adjusted his feed accordingly.

With billions of active users on social media, the amount of content can be overwhelming. To keep a user's feed relevant, the algorithms rank what each user sees based on his or her habits. Then they show content aligned with those interests. The unintended side effect of this is what Pariser called a filter bubble. "Your filter bubble is your own personal, unique universe of information that you live in online. And what's in your filter bubble depends on who you are, and it depends on what you do," said Pariser. "But the thing is that you don't decide what gets in. And more importantly, you don't actually see what gets edited out."[3]

PERSONALIZED RESULTS

Algorithms are not limited to social media. Other online services use them too, such as Google. Google tracks how a user behaves when searching for content. Its algorithm then uses that information to rank search results. This means that even though two people may search for the same keyword, they may get different search results. And online news sites, such as the *New York Times* and the *Washington Post*, have also experimented with this model. They can customize their home pages to feature stories most relevant to a specific user based on his or her history. The result of all this personalization is that each user begins to have a different reality. People see different information based solely on the data that algorithms have collected.

FLOCKING TOGETHER

Filter bubbles are also referred to as echo chambers and silos. They amplify what social scientists call homophily. This is the tendency for people to surround themselves with others who are like-minded. People with strong views on an issue tend to group together. When these issues are heated, as with politics or religion, algorithms push people with differing views further apart. The result is that people in these groups become increasingly isolated from those with other beliefs. They have little or no exposure to opinions that differ from their own.

Filippo Menczer is a network scientist at Indiana University. In his work, he tracks social media activity and how it polarizes people. "Conservatives are more likely to retweet tweets from other conservative people, and liberal people are more likely to retweet other liberal people, but there is very little stuff that goes across between the two," says Menczer. "And if you are a fringe or an extremist or somebody who believes in conspiracy, it is very easy for you to find other people like you and to form critical mass.

The polarization on social media can spill over into real-world political disputes and arguments.

So the network will give me the impression that most people—those that I'm connected with—agree with me."[4]

The result is that people create their own personalized reality based on information that may or may not accurately reflect wider reality. The stories, images, and posts they see often reinforce the beliefs they already hold. In some cases, this fosters intolerance, distrust, and hatred between groups. The speed with which social media is shared means these feelings become widespread very rapidly. The growth of social media has been so massive and so fast that ethics around algorithms haven't

"I LIKE TO SAY ALGORITHMS ARE OPINIONS EMBEDDED IN CODE, AND THAT ALGORITHMS ARE NOT OBJECTIVE. ALGORITHMS ARE OPTIMIZED TO SOME DEFINITION OF SUCCESS."[6]

—CATHY O'NEIL, COMPUTER SCIENTIST AND TECH WRITER

THE POWER OF ALGORITHMS

In 2014, a group of professors set out to learn just how much influence social media algorithms had on a user's experience. To do this, they created an app called FeedVis. They gave the app to study participants. It had a split screen. On the right was the standard news feed. On the left was a stream that had only posts from friends. Comparing the two feeds side by side shocked the study's participants. Most said they had no idea that an algorithm automatically generated their feed. It was eye-opening to many of them, who had believed what they had been seeing was a simple chronological feed.

caught up to the reality. But it doesn't have to stay this way.

Jesse Lehrich is a cofounder of Accountable Tech, a nonprofit dedicated to stopping the spread of misinformation on social media. For Lehrich, the solution is not smarter, more sophisticated algorithms. Instead, it's about handing control back to users. "What if people could say, 'I want to see news from a broad political spectrum of sources,' or 'I only want to see posts from friends and family'?" asked Lehrich.[5] This may be the way of social media in the future, but for now, the algorithms reign supreme.

MORE TO THE STORY

THE RISE OF SMARTPHONES AND APPS

For most of their early years, Facebook and other social media services could only be accessed on desktop or laptop computers. The rise of smartphone technology propelled the increasing use of social media. Smartphones had been around since the early 2000s, but they had not caught on with the masses. Early smartphones were expensive, hard to use, and often geared toward businesspeople. That all changed in 2007 when Apple CEO Steve Jobs unveiled the first iPhone. Unlike previous attempts at smartphones, the iPhone appealed to a wider audience. It allowed users to take pictures, connect to the internet, send texts and emails, and watch videos all from their phones. The design was simple, clean, and easy to use. The iPhone was expensive compared to other phones at the time, but it still caught on quickly. Google's competing Android smartphone platform launched in 2008. Third-party developers began scrambling to make smartphone apps.

In July 2008, Facebook launched the first version of its app. People no longer needed a desktop computer to scroll through Facebook. They could look at it on their phones at any time. As smartphones became more common, the number of Facebook users also increased. By January 2021, nearly all of Facebook's users had accessed the service through its mobile app.

CHAPTER SIX

HARVESTING DATA

In 2018, data consultant Christopher Wylie found himself at the center of a data privacy storm. "We exploited Facebook to harvest millions of people's profiles. And built models to exploit what we knew about them and target their inner demons," said Wylie.[1] His admissions would shock millions of Americans who suddenly realized their private data had been used for years without their knowledge or consent.

Back in 2013, Wylie helped found Cambridge Analytica. It was an international business that analyzed data for politicians. Wylie began working with an American conservative activist named Steve Bannon in 2014. Bannon thought of politics like war, and he wanted a new weapon that Wylie could provide.

Christopher Wylie's company, Cambridge Analytica, became a household name after its involvement in the 2016 presidential election.

"We were going to combine microtargeting, which had existed in politics, and was in part my background, but bring on board new constructs from psychology, so that we wouldn't just be targeting you as a voter, we'd be targeting you as a personality," explained Wylie.[2]

The plan was to collect massive amounts of data on Americans. Then that data could be used to influence voters on social media. American billionaire Robert Mercer invested $15 million to get Bannon's project started. Wylie was ready to start working on it, but he faced one huge problem. He did not have access to enough data to analyze the entire population of a country. To find that data, he turned to Dr. Aleksandr Kogan.

MICROTARGETING

Microtargeting is a system used to market goods, products, or people. It has exploded in growth since the creation of social media. It is unlike traditional marketing that appears in newspapers or television ads. In those systems, one message is sent to a broad audience. The entire audience receives the same message. But microtargeting is different. It can tailor an ad to specific people in a way that will be most relevant to them. That means people in different places receive different ads. Microtargeting is often highly effective. But it has a downside too. It can lead to the spread of misinformation and confusion about contentious topics, such as politics. It has the potential to segment people into different groups, creating divisions.

FRAGMENTING SOCIETY

Kogan was a Russian American psychology professor at

Cambridge University in England. He agreed to build an app to help Wylie harvest data from Facebook. Kogan would get to keep the data for his own use. The app, called "thisisyourdigitallife," was a personality quiz. As Facebook understood it, Kogan would be using the data for academic purposes only, so he had special permission to collect that data. The app not only harvested data from its users but also harvested data from the profiles of people in their network of friends. It was an efficient,

Aleksandr Kogan was a key figure in the Cambridge Analytica scandal.

simple way to gather huge amounts of data. But it was also highly deceptive.

"If you were a friend of somebody who used the app, you would have no idea that I've just pulled all of your data," said Wylie.[3] That data included everything on a person's profile, as well as status updates, "likes," and even private messages. In less than three months, Cambridge Analytica harvested more than 60 million profiles.[4]

With all these profiles, Cambridge Analytica built powerful algorithms. Those algorithms targeted voters with amazing precision and without the users' awareness. They knew what type of message would likely affect each voter in terms of topic, tone, and content. But that was not all. The algorithms could even predict how many times it would take users to see this type of material before they changed their opinions.

DATA CENTER ALLEY

The data that social media companies collect from their users must be stored somewhere. For this the companies use locations called data centers, buildings filled with computers that store data and are connected to the internet. The unofficial data capital of the world is in Ashburn, Virginia. It is referred to as Data Center Alley. Each day, approximately 70 percent of the world's internet traffic travels through Data Center Alley.[5]

Wylie ultimately began to see problems with what

he and others at Cambridge Analytica were doing. And those problems were much larger than just taking data without permission. They were problems that could permanently affect society. "Instead of standing in the public square and saying what you think and then letting people come and listen to you and have that shared experience as to what your narrative is, you are whispering into the ear of each and every voter, and you may be whispering one thing to this voter and another thing to another voter," said Wylie. "We risk fragmenting society in a way where we don't have any more shared experiences and we don't have any more shared understanding."[6]

PRIVACY CONCERNS

After the Cambridge Analytica story broke in 2018, Americans began looking at social media with a new lens. Many are wary of what social media companies know about them and what the companies do with that data. In a 2019 survey, more than 80 percent of Americans said they felt they had little control over their personal data. More than half were uncertain of what social media companies did with their personal data. While 97 precent of Americans agree to privacy policies for online services, less than 9 percent of Americans always read the policies to see what is included in them.[7]

LAWMAKERS GET INVOLVED

After Wylie came forward, Americans demanded answers. Lawmakers John Thune and Chuck Grassley scheduled a Senate hearing on the matter. "Social media has revolutionized the way we communicate, using data to connect people from around the world," said Grassley. "With all of the data exchanged over Facebook and other platforms, users deserve to know how their information is shared and secured. This hearing will explore approaches to privacy that satisfy consumer expectations while encouraging innovation."[8]

On April 10, 2018, Zuckerberg testified before lawmakers about his company's role in the Cambridge Analytica

"THE INDEPENDENCE OF CYBERSPACE"

Seeking to keep government regulation off the internet is a recurring battle. One of the most outspoken people in this fight was John Perry Barlow. He was a writer, political activist, and libertarian. Barlow was passionate about protecting the rights of people in the digital world. In 1996, the US government passed a law called the Communications Decency Act. It regulated internet content. Barlow and others saw it as a violation of the First Amendment right to free speech. Barlow wrote a scathing essay called "A Declaration of the Independence of Cyberspace." In it, he blasted government leaders for trying to regulate speech on the internet. "Governments of the Industrial World, you weary giants of flesh and steel, I come from Cyberspace, the new home of Mind," wrote Barlow. "On behalf of the future, I ask you of the past to leave us alone. You are not welcome among us. You have no sovereignty where we gather."[9]

scandal. In his opening statements, he told committee members that Facebook had taken steps to prevent this type of data breach from happening again. It investigated apps that had access to large amounts of data. And the company also allowed users to see what apps could access their personal data. The Federal Trade Commission ultimately fined Facebook $5 million.

For most of its history, the internet has been unregulated by the US government. It was hailed as a free, democratic space. It was designed without one central authority to control it. Early tech experts saw it as a utopia, a place where information could be exchanged freely. But growing internet companies soon realized they needed to make money to stay online. In the process, big tech companies such as Google, Amazon, and Facebook collected data on millions of users, and that data was valuable.

"WHEN AN ONLINE SERVICE IS FREE, YOU'RE NOT THE CUSTOMER—YOU'RE THE PRODUCT."[10]

—TIM COOK, CEO OF APPLE

CHAPTER SEVEN

FALSE STORIES

In late October 2016, news stories about a pizzeria in Washington, DC, began to circulate on social media. The stories claimed that a local pizzeria called Comet Ping Pong was the headquarters of a child-trafficking ring. The stories spread widely on Twitter, Instagram, Facebook, and elsewhere. They tied the child-trafficking ring to Hillary Clinton. At the time, Clinton was in the middle of a heated campaign for the presidency against Donald Trump.

In the following weeks, the stories continued to spread. The owner of Comet Ping Pong, James Alefantis, began to receive disturbing messages. People started posting messages on the pizzeria's social media

Events in late 2016 turned Comet Ping Pong from a simple pizzeria into a symbol of the harm that can be caused by the spread of misinformation online.

COMET
SMALL BUSINESS
SATURDAY

pages, including "we're on to you" and "I will kill you personally." Alefantis sought help from the police and the Federal Bureau of Investigation (FBI). He asked social media platforms to remove the stories. None of the efforts helped. The stories continued to spread unchecked, even though they were entirely false.

"From this insane, fabricated conspiracy theory, we've come under constant assault," said Alefantis.[1] Soon the situation progressed beyond just Alefantis receiving threatening messages. People began to target restaurant

Pizzeria owner James Alefantis found himself at the center of the national conversation around the dangers of online conspiracy theories.

employees and anyone who had liked or commented on the pizzeria's social media pages. Some people came to the restaurant to do their own investigations. One of those people was a 28-year-old North Carolina man named Edgar Welch.

On the afternoon of December 4, Welch entered the pizzeria with an assault rifle. His goal was to free children whom he believed were being held against their will. He shot the rifle at the lock on a closet door, where he believed the children may have been hidden. All that was in the closet was a computer. No one was injured, and Welch was taken into custody and later sentenced to prison.

The events centered on Comet Ping Pong became known as Pizzagate. For many Americans, Pizzagate served as a warning of what could happen when false news spread across social media unchecked. "What happened today demonstrates that promoting false and reckless conspiracy theories comes with consequences," Alefantis said. "I hope that those involved in fanning these flames will take a moment to contemplate what happened here today and stop promoting these falsehoods right away."[2]

HOW FALSE NEWS SPREADS

Millions of people across the world read news on social media every day. These platforms make it easy to find the day's top stories in one convenient place. But assessing whether these stories are true is not so easy. This is a major concern, since a growing number of Americans get their news from social media. In 2021, the Pew Research Center found that more than half of Americans—53 percent—regularly used social media as a news source. The top three sites they went to for news were Facebook, YouTube, and Twitter.[3]

Many of the news stories people see are presented to them by the platform's algorithms. Those algorithms do not look at factual content

SECTION 230

Social media companies have a special kind of legal protection from responsibility for spreading false stories. It is part of the Communications Decency Act of 1996. Section 230 of that law states, "No provider or user of an interactive computer service shall be treated as the publisher or speaker of any information provided by another information content provider."[4] That means social media sites are not responsible for what people post. The law makes social media sites and other platforms a vessel for transmitting information. They have no legal responsibility to make sure the stories are accurate or true. Supporters of the law see it as a guarantee of free speech online. Critics would like to see the law changed. They argue that when the law was made, no one imagined what kind of power viral stories on social media would have on society.

Algorithms have the potential to draw users of social media into the world of fake news stories.

of a story. Instead, they look at what a user has liked or interacted with in the past. While the origins of Pizzagate are murky, how the story spread is not. As conspiracy groups increasingly shared Pizzagate news, the stories drew the attention of social media algorithms. From there, the story jumped from conspiracy groups to other users.

"If a user . . . had indicated to Facebook's algorithms in some way that they were prone to believe in conspiracy theories, Facebook's recommendation engine would serve them Pizzagate groups," said Renée DiResta, manager at Stanford Internet Observatory. "This is an example of a conspiracy theory that was propagated across all social networks. The social network's own recommendation engine is voluntarily serving this up to people who had never searched for the term 'Pizzagate' in their life."[5]

LIES MOVE FASTER THAN TRUTHS

Algorithms aren't the only factor in the spread of false stories. A 2018 study at the Massachusetts Institute of Technology (MIT) showed that falsehoods tend to travel faster than truths. To determine this, scientists looked at 126,000 news story cascades on Twitter from 2006 to 2017. A cascade occurs when a tweet is shared repeatedly by different users, causing it to reach very broad networks of people. The cascades the researchers examined included more than 4.5 million tweets by approximately 3 million people.[6] The scientists used independent fact-checking organizations to determine whether the stories were true or false. Then they examined the data.

SYNTHETIC MEDIA

False news stories are just the starting point for misinformation. New forms of technology make determining what is true and false even more difficult. Among these technologies are synthetic media, also known as deepfakes. People can use computer programs to create realistic artificial audio and video recordings. As the technology improves, people may begin to have a hard time detecting whether a message is legitimate.

The MIT study revealed that false stories were 70 percent more likely to be retweeted than true stories. They also discovered that a true story takes about six times longer to reach 1,500 people than a false story does. The scientists created a hypothesis based on these findings. They believed that false news stories contained a high degree of novelty. "False news is more novel, and people are more likely to share novel information," said Sinan Aral, one of the scientists who worked on the study. "People who share novel information are seen as being in the know."[7]

THE ROLE OF EMOTIONS

The MIT scientists who studied the spread of false news stories also looked at how emotions affect the spread of those stories. False stories produced surprise and disgust in readers. These emotions motivated people to share. With true stories, people responded with trust, anticipation, and sadness. These emotions are less likely to inspire a user to share a story.

Once a story starts to spread on social media, it is nearly impossible to stop it. In 2020, wildfires ravaged Oregon. On Facebook and Twitter, false stories began to spread that left-wing protesters had started the fires. To battle back, local police departments took to social media and pleaded with people to stop spreading the false news. Ultimately, Facebook put warnings by fact-checkers on the

posts. And the FBI debunked the story officially. But by then it was too late. The false stories had been spreading for days.

The solution, according to many experts, is not to take down the false posts but to stop them before they go viral. Some people suggest looking to the stock market for inspiration. If stocks suddenly drop by a certain percentage, trading automatically stops. It gives traders a break to catch up on what is happening and make decisions based on that information. It could work similarly with false stories on social media. If a potentially false story looks like it is going viral, a social media service could block the post from being shared temporarily. This would stop a story from spreading until it is fact-checked.

CHALLENGES OF STOPPING THE SPREAD

Correcting false news once it goes viral is rarely successful. The *New York Times*, the *Washington Post*, and the fact-checking website Snopes all debunked the false stories about Comet Ping Pong. But that only made conspiracy theorists more passionate. Hours after these mainstream media posts appeared, a user on Twitter warned that they were fake. The tweet was posted by a man named Steven Smith, who claimed to be a representative of the 15th District of Georgia. The man did not exist, nor did the district he supposedly represented, yet the story was retweeted many times. On YouTube, a video that attempted to disprove the *New York Times* article was viewed widely and reposted on Facebook and Twitter. At that point, the original story about Comet Ping Pong spawned new stories. Conspiracy theorists claimed that the child-trafficking ring had a worldwide presence.

Today's global networks make it possible for false or misleading information to spread rapidly around the world.

FROM THE HEADLINES

FLAT-EARTHERS

In 2017, NBA player Kyrie Irving revealed on a podcast that he believed Earth was flat. "Can you really think of us rotating around the sun and all planets aligned, rotating in specific dates, being perpendicular with what's going on with these planets?" Irving asked. "The truth is right there. You've just got to go searching for it."[8] Irving was not alone in his beliefs. He, like hundreds of others, had discovered the Flat Earth Movement on YouTube. It is a conspiracy theory that Earth is a flat disc. The movement gained traction between 2015 and 2016. At the time, algorithms pushed flat-Earth videos on the "recommended" portion of the site. That's because the videos had a track record of hooking viewers. This meant YouTube could sell more ads on those videos. But just because a video had lots of recommendations did not make it true. Irving later apologized for his comments, and he explained how it all happened by saying, "You click a YouTube link and it's like how deep does the rabbit hole go?"[9]

Basketball star Kyrie Irving was among the high-profile celebrities who expressed support for the Flat Earth Movement.

CHAPTER EIGHT

FREEDOM OF SPEECH

Since joining Twitter in 2009, Donald Trump had amassed more than 88 million followers on his personal account, @RealDonaldTrump. As president, Trump's tweets became one of his most-used forms of communication. During his four years in office, Trump tweeted approximately 26,000 times. That averages to about 18 tweets per day.[1] Early in Trump's term, his press secretary, Sean Spicer, confirmed that Trump's tweets should be "considered official statements by the President of the United States."[2]

That is the way most of the nation treated them for Trump's term. Tweeting allowed Trump to bypass mainstream media, which he often said covered him unfairly. By tweeting, he could communicate directly

Twitter became one of President Donald Trump's preferred methods of communicating his thoughts to the American people.

Donald J. Trump
@realDonaldTrump
45th President of the United Sta
America

with his followers. Many of his tweets were controversial. For example, Trump accused the Speaker of the House of Representatives, Nancy Pelosi, of treason. He insulted Republicans who opposed him. And he retweeted posts from nearly 150 accounts that promoted content described by mainstream news sources as fringe or conspiratorial.

TWO DIFFERENT APPROACHES

In fall 2019, Facebook and Twitter faced pressure to begin fact-checking political ads to stop the spread of false news. Each platform took a different approach. Zuckerberg announced that Facebook would not subject any political ads to fact-checking. "We don't do this to help politicians, but because we think people should be able to see for themselves what politicians are saying. . . . I know many people disagree, but, in general, I don't think it's right for a private company to censor politicians or the news in a democracy," said Zuckerberg.[3] Twitter president Jack Dorsey took an opposing view. He announced the site would ban political ads. "While internet advertising is incredibly powerful and very effective for commercial advertisers, that power brings significant risks to politics, where it can be used to influence votes to affect the lives of millions," said Dorsey.[4]

Social media platforms allowed Trump to speak his mind without being filtered. He was not alone. Twitter, Facebook, and other platforms granted greater freedom of speech to world leaders than to normal users. This was allowed under a policy known as the newsworthiness exception. It meant that anything a world leader said could be considered news. Platforms could ban ordinary users for breaking their rules. The newsworthiness exception allowed leaders to post things that other users could be banned for posting. But that hands-off approach would test the limits of free speech on social media in 2020 and 2021.

TWITTER

Twitter is a microblogging social media site. It was created by programmers Jack Dorsey, Evan Williams, and Biz Stone in 2006. Twitter allows users to share short posts called tweets. It quickly gained a following of celebrities, business leaders, and politicians. Twitter became known for the breaking news stories its users posted. It was a trailblazer in using short posts—first limited to 140 characters and later to 280 characters—to quickly deliver messages. The site also pioneered the concept of using a hashtag before a keyword or topic on posts. This made it easier to find relevant posts on the site. Words that are hashtagged repeatedly may be categorized as trending topics on the site.

THE 2020 ELECTION AND ITS AFTERMATH

Donald Trump and Joe Biden faced off in the 2020 presidential election. It was a challenging campaign. The COVID-19 pandemic had spread to millions of people around the world. Racial tensions flared after a Black man named George Floyd was murdered by police in Minneapolis, Minnesota. False stories about COVID-19, the Black Lives Matter movement, the QAnon conspiracy theory, and the left-wing militant antifa movement spread virally on social media. The nation appeared more divided

MORE TO THE STORY

FREE SPEECH & FACT-CHECKING

The tension between free speech and social media rose in May 2020. That month, Twitter began labeling posts to indicate that they included misleading, disputed, or unverified claims. On May 26, Twitter added its first warning label to President Trump's account. It appeared on a pair of tweets that said, "There is NO WAY (ZERO!) that Mail-in Ballots will be anything less than substantially fraudulent. Mailboxes will be robbed, ballots will be forged & even illegally printed out & fraudulently signed. . . . This will be a Rigged Election. No way!"[5]

Users who clicked on the label found a statement from Twitter. It said, "On Tuesday, President Trump made a series of claims about potential voter fraud. . . . These claims are unsubstantiated, according to CNN, Washington Post and others. Experts say mail-in ballots are very rarely linked to voter fraud."[6] When Trump saw the warning he struck out at the platform, saying, "Twitter is completely stifling FREE SPEECH, and I, as President, will not allow it to happen."[7] The battle between Trump and Twitter continued following Election Day on November 3. Between Election Day and November 27, Twitter labeled 200 of Trump's tweets and retweets as containing misleading, false, or disputed information.

than it had been in recent memory. These turbulent times served as the backdrop for Americans when they voted in November 2020.

Biden won the election by seven million popular votes and received 306 electoral college votes. But Trump believed Biden had stolen the election from him through voter fraud. Trump filed legal cases to overturn the results in several states, but judges threw out the lawsuits in the absence of evidence. Trump did not give up. His social media posts encouraged his supporters to keep fighting for him. On December 18 he tweeted, "Statistically impossible to have lost the 2020 Election. Big protest in D.C. on January 6th. Be there, will be wild!"[8] A number of conservative groups organized on social media to attend the protest, united under the banner of #stopthesteal.

On Wednesday, January 6, 2021, Trump held a rally for his supporters. It took place a short distance from the Capitol as lawmakers prepared to certify the electoral votes. During his speech, Trump encouraged his supporters to march to the Capitol to stop the certification of electoral votes. He said he would join them, but he drove back to the White House instead. Those who

A large crowd of Trump supporters broke into the US Capitol on January 6, 2021.

marched to the Capitol were met by other protesters who had assembled there. The protestors then overpowered police, and the gathering became a riot. They breached the Capitol building, forcing the gathered lawmakers to run for safety and temporarily halting the certification of the electoral votes. Throughout the riot, participants posted photos and videos of the mayhem on social media. Five people died during the riot. Peace was restored later that night, and the certification of votes was completed.

THE FIRST AMENDMENT

On January 8, Twitter permanently suspended Trump's account. Company officials worried his tweets could lead to more violence. Twitter's official statement said, "Our public interest framework exists to enable the public to hear from elected officials and world leaders directly. It is built on a principle that the people have a right to hold power to account in the open. . . . However, we made it clear going back years that these accounts are not above our rules and cannot use Twitter to incite violence."[9] Facebook, Instagram, Snapchat, and other social media sites followed Twitter's lead by banning Trump.

THE FALLOUT

Across the world, people watched the US Capitol riot unfold on social media in real time. Some applauded the efforts of the protesters. Others were stunned by what they were witnessing. The authorities restored order three hours after the riot started. Twitter warned Trump not to post anything that could incite violence. That Friday, Trump tweeted, "The 75,000,000 great American Patriots who voted for me, AMERICA FIRST, and MAKE AMERICA GREAT AGAIN, will have a GIANT VOICE long into the future. They will not be disrespected or treated unfairly in any way, shape or form!!!"[10] Critics worried that his words could be interpreted as a call for more violence.

FROM THE HEADLINES

PARLER

When mainstream social media began to add warning labels to President Trump's posts, many of his supporters shifted to using Parler. The social media site launched in 2018, and it gained increased popularity in the aftermath of Election Day in 2020. On November 8, 2020—the day mainstream media reported Joe Biden as the winner of the 2020 election—Parler became the most-downloaded app for Apple and Android.

Parler billed itself as an unbiased social media platform where users could express themselves without fear of censorship. The site was criticized by many who felt it was being used to spread conspiracy theories and extremist views. Months later, it appeared that some people had used the site to plan the January 6 attack on the US Capitol. In an effort to prevent further violence, Apple and Google removed the app from their stores. Amazon, the host of Parler's digital infrastructure, refused to support the app any longer, and it went off-line on January 9, 2021, at 11:59 p.m. Closing the platform outraged users, who believed their speech was being censored. Parler came back online in February after finding an alternate host for its service.

The removal of the Parler app from the leading smartphone app stores drew praise from some and sharp criticism from others.

No SIM
9:04 AM
parler app
100%
PARLER
Read News, Speak Free
9:41
Feed
The Epochi Times
@epochtimes
Lee Cohen: "While most of the world is waylaid by the enormity of the pandemic, Britain and the United States have soldiered on with their planned trade negotiations this month."
64
63
352
See Comments
Elise Rhodes
@EliseRhodes

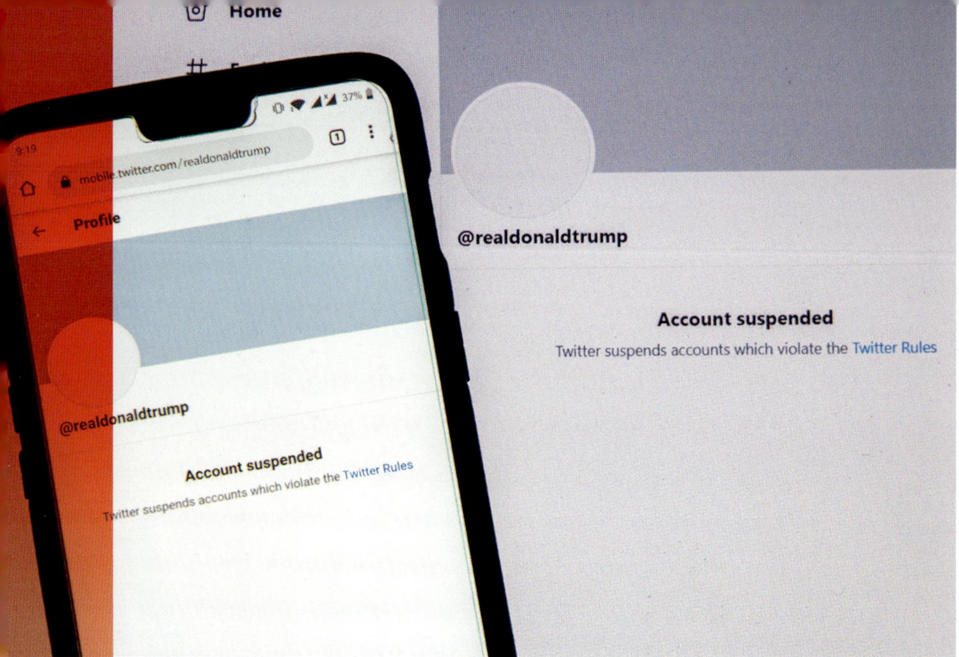

Twitter's decision to ban Trump from its service drew widespread criticism from conservatives.

Trump's supporters, including Representative Jim Jordan of Ohio, took to their own social media accounts to defend him. Jordan tweeted, "What happened on Wednesday at the U.S. Capitol is as wrong as wrong can be. But canceling conservative speech will not promote 'unity and healing.' It will only divide us further." Florida representative Matt Gaetz warned on his Twitter account that "Big tech tyranny is playing out before our very eyes."[11]

Many Trump supporters felt the bans were a violation of Trump's right of free speech. The First Amendment to the US Constitution guarantees that "Congress shall make no law . . . abridging the freedom of speech, or of the press."[12] The First Amendment is a safeguard. It prevents the government from punishing citizens for what they say or write. The amendment does have some limitations. It applies only to the government. It does not apply to private organizations, such as colleges, businesses, or landowners. The government does not own or run social media platforms. That means social media platforms are free to decide what information is or is not posted on their sites. Taking down a post or disabling a user is not a violation of Constitutional free speech.

"I THOUGHT ONCE EVERYBODY COULD SPEAK FREELY AND EXCHANGE INFORMATION AND IDEAS, THE WORLD IS AUTOMATICALLY GOING TO BE A BETTER PLACE. I WAS WRONG ABOUT THAT."[13]

— EVAN WILLIAMS, FOUNDER OF TWITTER

CHAPTER NINE

SOCIAL MEDIA TODAY

Social media is a place full of pressure to look good, have the right number of friends, and project an image of success. But keeping up this kind of appearance can be exhausting. Many social media users report harmful effects. These sites can lower self-esteem, cause stress, and weaken in-person relationships. For many, quitting social media helps alleviate these problems.

"Without [Instagram], I sleep better, my mind feels lighter," said a woman who identified herself only as Fanny. In the fall of 2020, she became one of the many people who have stepped away from social media. "I feel less anxious, less angry, and better able to organize my thoughts around what can be done with regard to

Many people have reported a sense of relief after quitting social media services.

al media
Delete "Instagram"?
eleting this app will also delete its
data, but any documents or data
stored in iCloud will not be deleted.
Cancel
Dele

social and political injustices rather than just being mad. I feel the gloom and doom is more manageable. And my friends are supportive. I have to make an added effort to check in with them via text, which feels more meaningful to me."[1]

Others who have stepped back from social media have decided they miss the connection with people that it provides. So much of modern life is shared through social media that people can feel out of touch without regularly logging in to these services. But those who choose to return often engage with it in a new way. For some, that means choosing to use only one platform rather than several or dedicating a specific time of day to using social media. For others, it means paring down lists of friends or turning off notifications to avoid distractions.

SCREEN TIME

For many people, recognizing and controlling how much time they spend on their phones is not an easy task. To help users, Apple introduced a feature known as Screen Time in 2018. It provides weekly reports of how much time users spend on their phones, as well as what apps they use most. The feature allows users to set time limits on apps. And it gives users a way to control notifications, so they provide fewer interruptions throughout the day. Similar features are available on phones from other manufacturers.

A LIFELINE

When the COVID-19 pandemic began to shut down cities in March 2020, many Americans began to reexamine their use of social media. They could not connect with friends at restaurants, parties, or theaters. Instead, people were confined to their homes. Social media was no longer just a way to mindlessly pass the time. For many, it became

For many people, sharing their pandemic experiences on social media helped them feel more connected to friends during a difficult time.

THE DIGITAL DIVIDE

Online services, including social media, have been life changing for billions of people around the world. But using those services requires access to a computer and an internet connection. The price for this access has come down over the years, but many people still lack the resources or technical skills to get online. Some people live in rural areas that aren't serviced by high-speed internet providers. The resulting gap between those who are online and those who are not has become known as the digital divide. As more aspects of daily life move online, including banking, school, and work, the digital divide means that many people may be left behind. The COVID-19 pandemic drove even more activity online, creating a disadvantage for students and workers without internet access.

a lifeline to friends and family members, as well as a source of news. People relied on social media in ways they had not in the past.

For some, social media became a way to beat loneliness, share their daily lives in new ways, and seek comfort. "The ability to connect via so many platforms not only helps alleviate feelings of isolation but increases the sense of psychological comfort," says Pamela Rutledge, director of the Media Psychology Research Center. "It makes people feel less lonely and less fearful to know they aren't dealing with this alone."[2]

Pandemic posts also had a different tone. Many of the carefully edited pictures showing a polished, ideal lifestyle gave way to more authentic posts. People shared stories of mental health struggles, video-chat mishaps, and the challenges of balancing working from home and online school. Social media had become a way to connect more honestly. People shared real struggles, laughed at them together, and connected amid a world of uncertainty.

For some, however, social media became a source of stress rather than comfort. Constant news updates, bickering about politics, and false information made social media unappealing. Some found posts too light amid the troubles of the world. "'Look at me doing my Peloton workout' or 'Look at me, I got in shape,'" said an anonymous social media user in a mocking voice. "Do you realize half a million people died? It feels so silly to show happy stories in a pandemic. Everything feels inappropriate."[3]

DOOMSCROLLING

As 2020 progressed, it led to a new term that became popular online: doomscrolling. It describes the act of scrolling through social media and reading story after story of bad news. And 2020 and early 2021 provided plenty of source material. People doomscrolled through months of lockdowns, overtaxed medical facilities, racial tensions, a divisive election, and an insurrection at the US Capitol. These stories were often dramatic and compelling, capturing users' attention. But too much doomscrolling can cause stress, anxiety, and sleeping problems. Experts recommend limiting this use of social media to five to 15 minutes per session. This allows a user to be informed without being flooded with bad news.

THE FUTURE OF SOCIAL MEDIA

Even for those who don't log on, the impact of social media is present throughout the world. Billions of people use social media platforms each day. The stories they read, the communities they join, and the videos they watch may be virtual, but the effects are real. While some of those effects are positive, many are not. It is a massive experiment in social interaction that often highlights both the best and the worst in society. Social media has shown the potential to alter society in ways that seemed unimaginable just a few decades ago.

Jaron Lanier is one of many tech thinkers who anticipates danger if social media platforms don't make changes. Lanier is a computer scientist and writer who has worked for some of the biggest names in tech, including Microsoft and Google. He also was one of the pioneers of virtual reality. His tech background has allowed him to see what goes on behind the scenes. "If we go down the current status quo for, let's say, another 20 years, we probably destroy our civilization through willful ignorance," said Lanier. "We probably degrade the world's

Jaron Lanier has been one of the most prominent voices drawing attention to the risks and dangers of social media.

democracies so that they fall into some sort of bizarre autocratic dysfunction. We probably ruin the global economy."[4]

While Lanier's prediction sounds grim, it's not inevitable. Humans built social media platforms, and humans can change them. Many tech insiders believe it all comes down to money. Social media companies profit from the data users provide. If that business model were to become less profitable, it could alter how the companies operate. One way to do that would be to create regulations. Few regulations exist for social media companies. For the most part, these companies regulate themselves. They make decisions that affect world events, but they are largely not accountable to the people affected by those decisions. Their only accountability is to shareholders who expect a profit.

Many former tech insiders who left the industry due to ethical concerns believe regulations are the way to provide accountability. One of those people is Joe Toscano. He is a former experience designer at Google and thinks regulations tied to money are the most promising way forward. "We could tax data collection and processing,

The decisions of today's individual users will help shape the future of social media and its effects on society.

the same way that you, for example, pay your water bill by monitoring the amount of water that you use," said Toscano. "You tax these companies on the data assets that they have. It gives them a fiscal reason to not acquire every piece of data on the planet."[5]

To that end, the US Congress has held several hearings with social media companies. Lawmakers are learning more about how the platforms work and how to protect the people who use them. Social media is neither inherently good nor inherently bad—it's just a tool for connection. It has the potential to improve the world or cause great harm. In its short existence, social media has done both. To many technology experts, how people choose to use this tool will determine society's future.

GRETA THUNBERG AND SOCIAL MEDIA

Many people use social media to speak out about social causes that are important to them. Among the most prominent is Greta Thunberg, a Swedish climate change and environmental activist. Thunberg captured the world's attention as an outspoken teenage activist in the late 2010s. She also built up a sizable presence on social media, amassing more than 5 million Twitter followers and nearly 12 million Instagram followers by 2021. She used her account to share pictures, videos, and news stories that underscore her messages about climate change. Thunberg and other modern activists have found social media to be an invaluable tool in spreading the word about their chosen issues.

ESSENTIAL FACTS

MAJOR EVENTS

- In May 1997, developer Andrew Weinreich launches SixDegrees, which is the first modern social media site. It is followed by others, including Friendster and Myspace. In 2004, Mark Zuckerberg launches Facebook. By 2008 it becomes the world's largest social media site.
- In 2018, Mark Zuckerberg testifies before the US Congress regarding data shared from user profiles through the company Cambridge Analytica. The data breach alarmed many users, illuminating the dark side of social media on a vast scale.
- In 2020, false stories spread rapidly across social media amid a global pandemic, racial unrest, and a heated presidential election. The speech that is allowed on social media and who determines what is allowed become hot-button issues with users. Some believe their right to free speech is being violated, while others accuse the social media companies of allowing false stories to spread virally.

KEY PLAYERS

- Mark Zuckerberg is the founder and CEO of Facebook.
- Tim Kendall is the former director of monetization at Facebook.
- Tristan Harris is a computer scientist, ethicist, and cofounder of the Center for Humane Technology.

IMPACT ON SOCIETY

Social media has grown at a rapid pace since the early 2000s, bringing with it many changes in how people relate to one another. It has made staying in touch with friends and family members much easier than in the past. People who may have few connections with others in their real-life communities can find like-minded people through social media. But not all of the changes are beneficial. Social media has been designed to addict users. News stories can go viral quickly, even if they are untrue. This has the potential to fracture society and breed mistrust between different groups. The technology has grown so quickly that it may take many years before laws, regulations, and ethics catch up to it.

QUOTE

"Social networks represent the digital reflection of what humans do: we connect and share."

—Jeremiah Owyang, leader and analyst in the tech industry

GLOSSARY

CENSOR

To impose values on others by limiting what they may read, write, hear, or see.

CHILD TRAFFICKING

A form of modern-day slavery that involves the trade and purchase of children for exploitation in forced labor and sexual slavery.

CONSPIRACY THEORY

A belief, without proof, that someone is responsible for an event or crime.

DECENTRALIZED

Spread out across several locations rather than contained in one central hub.

ETHICIST

A person who studies the rules of behavior based on ideas about what is morally good and bad.

HANDLE

A nickname used online.

LIBERTARIAN

One who believes in the doctrine of free will and upholding liberty in thought and action.

MAINSTREAM MEDIA

A collection of far-reaching news organizations that reflect and shape societal thought.

MONETIZE

To use a product or service to generate revenue.

PLATFORM

The website or other digital framework that makes it possible for an online service to function.

SHAREHOLDER

An individual or a group that owns parts of a company that are called shares.

VIRAL

Quickly gaining popularity and visibility online by spreading from person to person.

ADDITIONAL RESOURCES

SELECTED BIBLIOGRAPHY

Ferguson, Niall. *Niall Ferguson's Networld.* PBS, 2020.

Orlowski, Jeff, dir. *The Social Dilemma.* Exposure Labs, 2020.

Standage, Tom. *Writing on the Wall: Social Media, the First Two Thousand Years.* Bloomsbury, 2013.

FURTHER READINGS

Huddleston, Emma. *Using Social Media Responsibly.* Abdo, 2021.

Mooney, Carla. *Addicted to Social Media.* ReferencePoint Press, 2020.

Radley, Gail. *Facebook.* Abdo, 2019.

ONLINE RESOURCES

Booklinks
NONFICTION NETWORK
FREE! ONLINE NONFICTION RESOURCES

To learn more about social media and modern society, please visit **abdobooklinks.com** or scan this QR code. These links are routinely monitored and updated to provide the most current information available.

MORE INFORMATION

For more information on this subject, contact or visit the following organizations:

Facebook
1 Hacker Way
Menlo Park, CA 94025
650-308-7300
about.facebook.com
Facebook is the largest social media service on the planet. Its website includes information about the company, its platform, and how people use Facebook today.

Twitter
1355 Market St., Ste. 900
San Francisco, CA 94103
415-222-9670
about.twitter.com
Twitter is a prominent social media service that specializes in sharing short messages and links. Its website includes information about the company and how it approaches the societal challenges of social media.

SOURCE NOTES

CHAPTER 1. A TECH REVOLUTION

1. "Humans of New York Creator Brandon Stanton Shares the Secrets of His Craft." *YouTube*, uploaded by The Profile with Polina, 20 Oct. 2020, youtube.com. Accessed 10 Sept. 2021.

2. "Brandon Stanton: The Hard Work of Dreams." *The Chase Jarvis Live Show*, 21 Feb. 2014, chasejarvis.com.

3. "Humans of New York Creator Brandon Stanton Shares the Secrets of His Craft."

4. "Facebook Reports Fourth Quarter and Full Year 2020 Results." *Facebook Investor Relations*, 27 Jan. 2021, investor.fb.com. Accessed 30 July 2021.

5. John Gramlich. "10 Facts about Americans and Facebook." *Pew Research Center*, 1 June 2021, pewresearch.org. Accessed 30 July 2021.

6. "Social Media Fact Sheet." *Pew Research Center*, 7 Apr. 2021, pewresearch.org. Accessed 30 July 2021.

7. David Shapiro Jr. "Human by Human, a Following Grows." *Wall Street Journal*, 14 Oct. 2013, wsj.com. Accessed 30 July 2021.

8. "The Revolution of Social Media for Business." *Om Infosolutions*, 20 Nov. 2017, ominfosolutions.com. Accessed 30 July 2021.

9. Amy Mitchell et al. "Many Americans Say Made-up News Is a Critical Problem." *Pew Research Center*, 5 June 2019, journalism.org. Accessed 30 July 2021.

10. @AmyJoMartin. "Social Media is the ultimate equalizer." *Twitter*, 23 Aug. 2016, 12:53 p.m., twitter.com.

CHAPTER 2. REMOVING THE BARRIERS OF DISTANCE AND TIME

1. Tom Standage. *The Victorian Internet: The Remarkable Story of the Telegraph and the Nineteenth Century's Online Pioneers*. Walker and Co., 1998. 46–48.

2. Tom Standage. *Writing on the Wall: Social Media, the First Two Thousand Years*. Bloomsbury, 2013. 182–183.

3. Willa Kane. "Frontier Diary: The Telegraph Changed Life in Glenwood Springs." *Frontier Historical Society and Museum*, 4 Aug. 2015, postindependent.com. Accessed 30 July 2021.

4. Clive Thompson. "Texting Isn't the First New Technology Thought to Impair Social Skills." *Smithsonian Magazine*, Mar. 2016, smithsonianmag.com. Accessed 30 July 2021.

5. Rebecca Onion. "A Telephone Map of the United States Shows Where You Could Call Using Ma Bell in 1910." *Slate*, 16 Mar. 2015, slate.com. Accessed 30 July 2021.

6. Standage, *Writing on the Wall*, 182–183.

7. Jesse Hicks. "Ray Tomlinson, the Inventor of Email: 'I See Email Being Used, by and Large, Exactly the Way I Envisioned.'" *The Verge*, 2 May 2012, theverge.com. Accessed 30 July 2021.

8. Michael Ray. "Social Network." *Encyclopedia Britannica*, n.d., britannica.com. Accessed 30 July 2021.

9. Janet Kornblum. "Teens Hang Out at MySpace." *USA Today*, 9 Jan. 2006, usatoday.com. Accessed 30 July 2021.

10. "Number of Active Users at Facebook Over the Years." *Yahoo*, 23 Oct. 2012, finance.yahoo.com. Accessed 30 July 2021.

CHAPTER 3. THE BENEFITS OF SOCIAL MEDIA

1. A. Pawlowski. "'Very Overwhelming': Woman Dubbed 'Burger King Baby' on Meeting Birth Mom." *Today*, 10 Apr. 2014, today.com. Accessed 30 July 2021.

2. Kevin Amerman. "'Burger King Baby' Finds the Birth Mom Who Abandoned Her." *Los Angeles Times*, 29 Mar. 2014, latimes.com. Accessed 30 July 2021.

3. Monica Anderson and Jingjing Jiang. "Teens, Social Media and Technology 2018." *Pew Research Center*, 31 May 2018, pewresearch.org. Accessed 30 July 2021.

4. *The Social Dilemma*. Directed by Jeff Orlowski, Exposure Labs, 2020.

5. Tom Standage. *Writing on the Wall: Social Media, the First Two Thousand Years*. Bloomsbury, 2013. 214.

6. Mark Zuckerberg. "Fifteen Years Ago Today, I Launched the First Version of the Facebook Website from My College Dorm." *Facebook*, 4 Feb. 2019, facebook.com. Accessed 30 July 2021.

7. "The Facebook Dilemma." *Frontline*, PBS, 2018.

8. Abby Ohlheiser. "The Woman Behind 'Me Too' Knew the Power of the Phrase When She Created It—10 Years Ago." *Washington Post*, 19 Oct. 2017, washingtonpost.com. Accessed 30 July 2021.

9. @Alyssa_Milano. "If you've been sexually harassed or assaulted." *Twitter*, 15 Oct. 2017, 3:21 p.m., twitter.com.

10. Joyce Chen. "Alyssa Milano Wants Her 'Me Too' Campaign to Elevate Harvey Weinstein Discussion." *Rolling Stone*, 17 Oct. 2017, rollingstone.com. Accessed 30 July 2021.

11. Emily Reaux. "Desperate Cries for Help Pouring in from Flood Victims." *WTSP*, 27 Aug. 2017, wtsp.com. Accessed 30 July 2021.

12. Maya Rhodan. "'Please Send Help.' Hurricane Harvey Victims Turn to Twitter and Facebook." *Time*, 30 Aug. 2017, time.com. Accessed 30 July 2021.

CHAPTER 4. THE ATTENTION ECONOMY

1. Tristan Harris. "How a Handful of Tech Companies Control Billions of Minds Every Day." *TED*, 28 July 2017, ted.com. Accessed 30 July 2021.

2. *The Social Dilemma*. Directed by Jeff Orlowski, Exposure Labs, 2020.

3. *The Social Dilemma*.

4. "Facebook Unveils Facebook Ads." *Facebook*, 6 Nov. 2007, about.fb.com. Accessed 30 July 2021.

5. *The Social Dilemma*.

6. Ben Gilbert. "Facebook Just Published a Message for Its Users: No, You're Not the Product." *Business Insider*, 23 Apr. 2018, businessinsider.com. Accessed 30 July 2021.

7. Hilary Andersson. "Social Media Apps Are 'Deliberately' Addictive to Users." *BBC*, 4 July 2018, bbc.co.uk. Accessed 30 July 2021.

8. James Vincent. "Former Facebook Exec Says Social Media Is Ripping Apart Society." *The Verge*, 11 Dec. 2017, theverge.com. Accessed 30 July 2021.

9. "Chamath Palihapitiya, Founder and CEO Social Capital, on Money as an Instrument of Change." *YouTube*, uploaded by Stanford Graduate School of Business, 13 Nov. 2017, youtube.com. Accessed 10 Sept. 2021.

10. Andersson, "Social Media Apps Are 'Deliberately' Addictive to Users."

SOURCE NOTES CONTINUED

11. Mike Allen. "Sean Parker Unloads on Facebook." *Axios*, 9 Nov. 2017, axios.com. Accessed 30 July 2021.

12. Ja'han Jones. "Jaron Lanier Helped Create Social Media, and Now He's Begging You to Leave It Behind." *Huffington Post*, 12 Dec. 2018, huffpost.com. Accessed 30 July 2021.

CHAPTER 5. ALGORITHMS

1. *The Social Dilemma*. Directed by Jeff Orlowski, Exposure Labs, 2020.

2. Holman W. Jenkins Jr. "Google and the Search for the Future." *Wall Street Journal*, 14 Aug. 2010, wsj.com. Accessed 30 July 2021.

3. Eli Pariser. "Beware of Online 'Filter Bubbles.'" *TED*, Mar. 2011, ted.com. Accessed 30 July 2021.

4. "Disruption." *Niall Ferguson's Networld*, PBS, 17 Mar. 2020.

5. Joanna Stern. "Social-Media Algorithms Rule How We See the World." *Wall Street Journal*, 17 Jan. 2021, wsj.com. Accessed 30 July 2021.

6. *The Social Dilemma*.

CHAPTER 6. HARVESTING DATA

1. Alexandra Ma and Ben Gilbert. "Facebook Understood How Dangerous the Trump-Linked Data Firm Cambridge Analytica Could Be." *Business Insider*, 23 Aug. 2019, businessinsider.com. Accessed 30 July 2021.

2. Carole Cadwalladr. "'I Made Steve Bannon's Psychological Warfare Tool': Meet the Data War Whistleblower." *Guardian*, 18 Mar. 2018, theguardian.com. Accessed 30 July 2021.

3. Cadwalladr, "Meet the Data War Whistleblower."

4. Cadwalladr, "Meet the Data War Whistleblower."

5. "Winner Takes All." *Niall Ferguson's Networld*, PBS, 17 Mar. 2020.

6. Cadwalladr, "Meet the Data War Whistleblower."

7. Brooke Auxier et al. "Americans and Privacy." *Pew Research Center*, 15 Nov. 2019, pewresearch.org. Accessed 30 July 2021.

8. "Facebook, Social Media Privacy, and the Use and Abuse of Data." *US Senate Committee on Commerce, Science, & Transportation*, 10 Apr. 2018, commerce.senate.gov. Accessed 30 July 2021.

9. John Perry Barlow. "A Declaration of the Independence of Cyberspace." *Electronic Frontier Foundation*, n.d., eff.org. Accessed 30 July 2021.

10. Ben Gilbert. "Facebook Just Published a Message for Its Users: No, You're Not the Product." *Business Insider*, 23 Apr. 2018, businessinsider.com. Accessed 30 July 2021.

CHAPTER 7. FALSE STORIES

1. Cecilia Kang. "Fact Check: This Pizzeria Is Not a Child Trafficking Site." *New York Times*, 22 Nov. 2016, nytimes.com. Accessed 30 July 2021.

2. Eric Lipton. "At a Pizzeria Harassed Online, a Man Is Held after Firing a Rifle." *New York Times*, 5 Dec. 2016, nytimes.com. Accessed 30 July 2021.

3. Elisa Shearer and Amy Mitchell. "News Use Across Social Media Platforms in 2020." *Pew Research Center*, 12 Jan. 2021, journalism.org. Accessed 30 July 2021.

4. "Section 230 of the Communications Decency Act." *Electronic Frontier Foundation*, n.d., eff.org. Accessed 30 July 2021.

5. *The Social Dilemma*. Directed by Jeff Orlowski, Exposure Labs, 2020.

6. Peter Dizikes. "Study: On Twitter, False News Travels Faster than True Stories." *MIT News*, 8 Mar. 2018, news.mit.edu. Accessed 30 July 2021.

7. Dizikes, "Study: On Twitter, False News Travels Faster than True Stories."

8. Chris Matyszczyk. "NBA Star Kyrie Irving Believes Earth Is Flat." *CNET*, 8 Feb. 2017, cnet.com. Accessed 30 July 2021.

9. Pete Blackburn. "Kyrie Irving Apologizes for Saying Earth Is Flat." *CBS Sports*, 1 Oct. 2018, cbssports.com. Accessed 30 July 2021.

CHAPTER 8. FREEDOM OF SPEECH

1. "Factbox—Trump Tweets Attacked Leaders and Businesses." *Reuters*, 8 Jan. 2021, reuters.com. Accessed 30 July 2021.

2. Elizabeth Landers. "White House: Trump's Tweets Are 'Official Statements.'" *CNN*, 6 June 2017, cnn.com. Accessed 30 July 2021.

3. "Mark Zuckerberg Stands for Voice and Free Expression." *Facebook*, 17 Oct. 2019, facebook.com. Accessed 30 July 2021.

4. @Jack. "We've made the decision to stop all political advertising on Twitter." *Twitter*, 30 Oct. 2019, 3:05 p.m., twitter.com.

5. Dan Mangan and Kevin Breuninger. "Twitter Fact-Checks Trump, Slaps Warning Labels on His Tweets about Mail-In Ballots." *CNBC*, 26 May 2020, cnbc.com. Accessed 30 July 2021.

6. "Trump Makes Unsubstantiated Claim That Mail-in Ballots Will Lead to Voter Fraud." *Twitter*, 26 May 2020, twitter.com. Accessed 30 July 2021.

7. Mangan and Breuninger, "Twitter Fact-Checks Trump."

8. Will Carless. "Nation's Capital Braces for Violence as Extremist Groups Converge to Protest Trump's Election Loss." *USA Today*, 4 Jan. 2021, usatoday.com. Accessed 30 July 2021.

9. "Permanent Suspension of @realDonaldTrump." *Twitter*, 8 Jan. 2021, blog.twitter.com. Accessed 30 July 2021.

10. Brian Fung. "Twitter Bans President Trump Permanently." *CNN*, 9 Jan. 2021, cnn.com. Accessed 30 July 2021.

11. Michael Ruiz. "Trump Supporters, Lawmakers React to Twitter Ban." *Fox News*, 8 Jan. 2021, foxnews.com. Accessed 30 July 2021.

12. Geoffrey R. Stone and Eugene Volokh. "Freedom of Speech and the Press." *Constitution Center*, n.d., constitutioncenter.org. Accessed 30 July 2021.

13. David Streitfeld. "'The Internet Is Broken': @ev Is Trying to Salvage It." *New York Times*, 20 May 2017, nytimes.com. Accessed 30 July 2021.

CHAPTER 9. SOCIAL MEDIA TODAY

1. Brittney Wong. "People Who Deleted Their Social Media Share What It's Like." *Huffington Post*, 20 Apr. 2021, huffpost.com. Accessed 30 July 2021.

2. Rani Molla. "Posting Less, Posting More, and Tired of It All: How the Pandemic Has Changed Social Media." *Vox*, 1 Mar. 2021, vox.com. Accessed 30 July 2021.

3. Molla, "Posting Less, Posting More, and Tired of It All."

4. *The Social Dilemma*. Directed by Jeff Orlowski, Exposure Labs, 2020.

5. *The Social Dilemma*.

INDEX

addiction, 13, 44–47
Advanced Research Projects Agency Network (ARPANET), 21–22
Alefantis, James, 66–69
algorithms, 40, 48–56, 62, 70–71, 72, 76
Amazon, 65, 86
Arab Spring, 32, 36

Bannon, Steve, 58–60
Barlow, John Perry, 64
Bell, Alexander Graham, 20
Ben Ali, Zine al-Abidine, 33
Berners-Lee, Tim, 23
Biden, Joe, 81, 83, 86
Burke, Tarana, 34

Cambridge Analytica, 58, 62–63, 64–65
cascades, 72
censorship, 80, 86
Center for Humane Technology, 38
Clinton, Hillary, 66
Communications Decency Act of 1996, 64, 70
COVID-19, 81, 93–95

data privacy, 11, 58, 63, 64
Deprill, Katheryn, 26–28
DiResta, Renée, 71–72
dopamine, 46
Dorsey, Jack, 80, 81

Facebook, 4–7, 9, 11, 25, 26–31, 32–33, 36, 37, 41–42, 43, 45–47, 48, 52, 57, 58, 61, 64–65, 66, 70, 71, 73, 75, 80, 85
false information, 10, 66–75, 76, 80, 81, 82, 95
Federal Bureau of Investigation (FBI), 68, 75
Federal Trade Commission, 65
filter bubbles, 52–53, 54
Fischer, Claude, 20
Flat Earth Movement, 76
Floyd, George, 81
free speech, 10, 64, 70, 81, 82, 88–89

Gaetz, Matt, 88
Ghonim, Wael, 32–33
Google, 40–41, 52, 53, 57, 65, 86, 96, 98
Grassley, Chuck, 64

Harris, Tristan, 38, 43
homophily, 54
Humans of New York (HONY), 4–7
Hurricane Harvey, 36–37

Instagram, 9, 31, 45, 66, 85, 90, 99
Irving, Kyrie, 76

Jordan, Jim, 85, 88

Karp, David, 7
Kendall, Tim, 29, 41
Kogan, Aleksandr, 60–61

Lanier, Jaron, 47, 96–97
Lehrich, Jesse, 56
LinkedIn, 24, 31

Massachusetts Institute of Technology (MIT), 72–73
Menczer, Filippo, 54–55
mental health, 12, 94, 95
microtargeting, 60
Milano, Alyssa, 34
monetization, 29, 40, 41, 42
Morse, Samuel, 16, 17, 18
Morse code, 18
Mosaic, 23
Mubarak, Hosni, 32–33
Myspace, 24–25, 34

newsworthiness exception, 80–81

Oregon wildfires, 73–75

Palihapitiya, Chamath, 46
Pariser, Eli, 52–53
Parker, Sean, 47
Parler, 86
Pelosi, Nancy, 80
Pew Research Center, 7, 28, 70
Pinterest, 7, 9, 29
Pizzagate, 66–69, 71–72

Raskin, Aza, 45, 47
Rutledge, Pamela, 94

Said, Khaled, 32
Seibert, Jeff, 50
SixDegrees, 24
smartphones, 57
Snapchat, 9, 85
Spicer, Sean, 78
Stanton, Brandon, 4–7
synthetic media, 72

telegraphs, 16, 17, 18–19, 20, 21
telephones, 20–21, 22
Thune, John, 64
Tomlinson, Raymond, 22
Toscano, Joe, 98–99
Trump, Donald, 66, 78–80, 81–88
Tumblr, 7
2020 election, 81–83, 86, 95
Twitter, 7, 9, 11, 31, 45, 50, 66, 70, 72, 73, 75, 78, 80, 81, 82, 85, 88, 89, 99

US Capitol riot, 84–85, 86, 88, 95
US Congress, 17, 43, 88, 99
USENET, 22
user data, 11, 41, 43, 50, 51, 53, 58–63, 64–65, 97
Usher, Nikki, 37

viral, 9, 10, 34, 70, 75, 81

WeChat, 9
Weinreich, Andrew, 24
Welch, Edgar, 69
Willis, Maritza Ritz, 36–37
World Wide Web, 23
Wylie, Christopher, 58–60, 61–63, 64

YouTube, 7, 31, 44, 45, 70, 75, 76

Zuckerberg, Mark, 25, 29–30, 41, 43, 64, 80

ABOUT THE AUTHOR

KATE CONLEY

Kate Conley has been writing nonfiction books for children for more than ten years. When she's not writing, Conley spends her time reading, sewing, and solving crossword puzzles. She lives in Minnesota with her husband and two children.

ABOUT THE CONSULTANT

ASTA ZELENKAUSKAITE, PhD

Asta Zelenkauskaite, PhD, is an associate professor of communication, affiliated with the Science, Technology, and Society program at Drexel University. She is also an affiliate with Vilnius Tech University, Lithuania. Dr. Zelenkauskaite's work focuses on emergent practices on mobile and social media, ranging from empowering practices to automated dark participation online.